INSPIRED TRAVELLER'S GUIDE
SPIRITUAL PLACES

INSPIRED
TRAVELLER'S GUIDE

SPIRITUAL PLACES

SARAH BAXTER

ILLUSTRATIONS BY
HARRY & ZANNA GOLDHAWK

Brimming with creative inspiration, how-to projects and useful information to enrich your everyday life, Quarto Knows is a favourite destination for those pursuing their interests and passions. Visit our site and dig deeper with our books into your area of interest: Quarto Creates, Quarto Cooks, Quarto Homes, Quarto Lives, Quarto Drives, Quarto Explores, Quarto Gifts, or Quarto Kids.

First published in 2018 by Aurum Press
an imprint of The Quarto Group
The Old Brewery, 6 Blundell Street
London N7 9BH
United Kingdom

www.QuartoKnows.com

A catalogue record for this book is available from the British Library.

ISBN 978 1 78131 742 6
Ebook ISBN 978 1 78131 774 7

10 9 8 7 6 5 4 3 2 1
2022 2021 2020 2019 2018

Typeset in Gill Sans
Design by Paileen Currie and Jayne Martin-Kaye

Printed in China

CONTENTS

INTRODUCTION

YOU STOP. Strain to listen. Yes, you are sure: the landscape is trying to speak. Walking across this rolling countryside, pocked with strange standing stones, you're certain you hear it. There is animation in every blade of grass, gossip amid the bushes, whispers on the wind. Every hump, bump, ridge and rise seems to be more than mere earth. It feels like spirits from another realm are thrusting through, eager to tell you their tales. If only you could tune in to their precise frequency. If only you could hear what the spectres swirling around this sacred spot are trying to say ...

There are certain places that manage to seep into your soul. They don't stop at delighting your external senses with their drama or design. No, they have a way of inching further; of permeating your skin and sinking deep, deep down inside; of making you ask new questions about yourself, maybe even about the crux of human existence.

These places might not be any more beautiful, striking, unusual or monumental than plenty of other great sites of the world – although often they are all of these things combined. But, somehow, they have more heft. And that's because they are sacred, carrying the beatific baggage of centuries – maybe millennia – of reverence by our forebears. They are places bolstered by the weight of a billion hopes and prayers.

When you visit a spiritual place, you are not simply admiring a cute quirk of geology or a clever bit of architectural engineering. While the Eiffel Tower is excellent, it won't send transcendent shivers down your spine. No, at a spiritual place you are also seeing and sensing the stories behind the rocks, bricks, mud and mortar. You are channelling the ancestors who have stood where you now stand, and the dreams and fears that they brought with them. No matter what your own faith or feeling, there's no denying that these holy sites have meant a great deal – maybe everything – to the hundreds, thousands, millions who have come before.

This book aims to transport you to a handful of these more-than-they-seem locations; places that are imbued with magic, mystery and a sprinkle of the divine. With the help of beautiful illustrations, the book evokes the essence of 25 separate spots around the planet, making their legends leap to life on the page. Flick through and, without leaving your armchair, you can travel across a range of religions and beliefs.

You can swoop across continents, fly over oceans, delve into mountain ranges, race across deserts and plunge into the heart of bustling cities. Spiritual places don't fit any one type – they are linked by the possession of a greater symbolism but not by their structure. In Haiti, for instance, followers of Catholicism-cum-vodou rush to a tiered waterfall cascading in the jungle to perform their prayers (page 126). Meanwhile, in Myanmar, Buddhists worship at a man-made tiered pagoda that soars up to the heavens and is slathered in gold (page 66). Natural, unnatural; beauty and divinity in different forms, but spiritual nonetheless.

Mother Nature has provided many important places of pilgrimage and power. Indeed, some of her creations wield such innate and abundant energy that humans have been unable to resist them. Whole mythologies have been based around particular mountains, there are lakes said to have engendered whole civilisations and there are rivers believed to be the very essence of life itself.

Take Mount Kailash in Tibet (page 80): regal, solitary, massive, magnificent, not to mention the source of Asia's most important waterways. How could mankind not imbue this forbidding behemoth of rock with otherworldly significance? You don't have to be Buddhist, Bon, Jain or Hindu to be moved by its sheer scale. But witnessing the adherents of those religions interact with their own visions of Mount Kailash, watching them prostrate and pray and weep in the presence of the peak, can elevate your emotional response to a higher level.

Other entries in this book focus on sites that have been specifically constructed for worship. Over the eons, humans have built untold numbers of temples, tabernacles, churches, monasteries, mosques, shrines, stupas, synagogues, pagodas and all manner of other holy places. Many of these sit on sites where the world was once upturned – where something of such import occurred that a marker was deemed essential. For instance, France's Sanctuary of Lourdes (page 38) is now a colossal pilgrimage complex that is visited by millions of devotees each year. It is packed with chapels, holy baths and shops touting votive candles and rosary beads. But the biggest queues are for the small, simple, miraculous cave where an innocent young girl had visions of the Virgin Mary. At its heart is still the place where the human once connected with the divine.

It doesn't matter where in the world you go, peoples throughout the ages have created their own sorts of sacred. Whether it's Native Americans trying to fathom life in the Wild West, Maori creating a mythology to fit volcanically volatile New Zealand or the Inca devising their own gods to oversee their South American empire, humans have always sought stories and systems to explain the world around them. By travelling – whether physically or through the pages of a book – you get to see the colourful, wonderful differences in these systems, but also the similarities that nod to a universal desire for order and explanation.

Of course, there are many more places that could have been included here. For instance, another chapter could have whisked you across the desert to Iran's Pir-e-Sabz fire temple, the most important Zoroastrian pilgrimage site, which clings to a craggy rock face and burns with an eternal flame. Yet another could have journeyed across the Tanzanian savannah to the curious cone of Ol Doinyo Lengai, a huff-puffing volcano that produces a strange sort of lava, and which the Maasai revere as the 'Mountain of God'. So many exciting, thrilling, faith-full, fascinating destinations that illustrate the ways that people through the ages have tried to make sense of our planet, and still do today. So many sacred stories still to be told ...

CAMINO DE SANTIAGO

PAUSE A moment. Touch your fingers to the rich Galician soil – trodden by feet just like yours for over a thousand years. If only this earth could speak of all those soles; of the monks, the paupers, the princes, the penitent, the desperate, the backpackers, the agnostics, the regular Joes. All walking for miles across Spain to reach the final resting place of St James, each making their pilgrimage along the Camino de Santiago for their own reasons. A journey of history, spirituality, community, adventure ...

The story of the Camino is as old as Christianity itself. Following Jesus's resurrection, St James became head of the Church. It's said he travelled from Jerusalem to Spain to spread the Word of Christ, then returned to the Holy Land where he was martyred. After his death, St James's body was allegedly sailed to northwestern Spain, and then buried – though the location of his tomb was soon lost.

Lost, that is, until the ninth century. Around AD 815, a hermit named Pelayo had a vision in which lights shone on a place in the woods of Mount Libredon. Further investigation uncovered a Roman-era tomb; St James's body lay inside. A church was built on the site, and the city of Santiago de Compostela grew around it. Pilgrims began to come; within 300 years, Santiago was Europe's premier pilgrimage site.

Peregrinos (pilgrims) came from across the continent, seeking salvation. Ways of St James spidered out from Santiago's beatific remains, with the route from France – known as the Camino Frances – becoming most popular. From St-Jean-Pied-de-Port,

just north of the Pyrenees, the trail to Santiago measures around 780 kilometres (485 miles).

Once over the Pyrenees, *peregrinos* headed west through what are now the provinces of Navarra and vine-streaked La Rioja, across Castile and León's endless *meseta* (high plateau), over the Cordillera Cantábrica and into the lush valleys of Galicia. Finally, after weeks or months of walking, *peregrinos* arrived at the Apostle's tomb.

The cathedral that houses the shrine today is a fitting finale. After the previous chapel was razed in 997, construction began on the current building in 1075. While the basic medieval structure remains, Romanesque, Gothic, Baroque and Neoclassical additions have been made. Standing in the wide Plaza del Obradoiro before the cathedral's exuberant Baroque facade of spires, filigree and St James statuary, even the most sceptical of pilgrims will feel their soul stir.

Entrance is via the Portal of Glory. On this doorway are carvings of the Last Judgement. Christ is in the middle, St James is just below. Since the Middle Ages pilgrims have prayed with their fingers pushed into the tree beneath St James – look closely and you will see the indents.

The sepulchre of St James lies beneath the main altar. Pilgrims circle along its right side to embrace the Apostle's image and view his remains. A pilgrim mass is held daily at noon; the priest begins by reading a list of all those who've been received in the Pilgrims' Office in the past 24 hours. It's the moment every *peregrino* has dreamed of. But it's not really the point.

No. While the Camino de Santiago has a definite destination, undertaking this iconic pilgrimage is about the journey. It's about rising to the challenges of keeping going day after day. It's about the meals, laughs and tears shared with fellow *peregrinos* as you bunk down together in *albergues* (pilgrim hostels) each night. It's about those simple, heart-soaring moments when Mother Nature does something spectacular, making you fully believe in a higher power. And it's about the realisation that reaching the finish is not the end. As pilgrims leave Santiago's cathedral through the south door, they see a Chi-Rho – the symbol of Christ. But the Greek letters are written backwards. The end has become the start. A new journey begins.

Santiago de
Compostela

Sarria

Melide

O Cebreiro

Samos

Ponferrada

Leó

Astorga

Portugal

France

St-Jean-Pied-de-Port

Roncesvalles

Estella

Pamplona

Carrión de
los Condes

Puente La Reina

Burgos

Logroño

Sahagún

Castrojeriz

Santo Domingo
de la Calzada

Spain

What?	Catholic cathedral inside a magnificent mosque, one of the world's finest buildings
Where?	Córdoba, Spain

LA MEZQUITA

THE SCENT of orange blossom infuses the air with a sweetness you can almost taste – a delicious aperitif to this feast of a building. Beyond the Mezquita's sun-dazzled, citrus-spritzed courtyard, those fruit trees melt into a man-made forest of columns and red-white candy-stripe arches that seems to stretch to the end of space. It's architecturally audacious. But it's also beautifully simple: no distracting frescoes or tombs, no neck-cricking high ceiling, just a glorious geometry of pillar after pillar, intersecting and interacting with the windows' light and shade. Serene and spacious, it's a spiritual oasis where the mind is unshackled from physical focus and free to wander in thought and prayer ...

'Mezquita' is Spanish for 'mosque'. But this striking complex in the Andalucían city of Córdoba is far too complicated to be summed up in one word. It's been many things to many people, not least an exquisite example of multi-faith harmony: there was a time when Muslims, Jews and Christians happily coexisted here.

A religious edifice has occupied this spot since the Romans erected a temple of Janus, god of beginnings and gateways. In the sixth century the Visigoths replaced it with the Basilica of San Vicente, remains of which can still be seen in the Mezquita's basement. After the Islamic conquest of Iberia at the beginning of the eighth century, the basilica was split in two and briefly shared by Muslims and Christians. Then in AD 784, Arab emir Abd ar-Rahman I purchased the lot and started constructing a grand new mosque, as befitting what was then one of the greatest cities of the medieval world.

The emir's masterpiece was divided into 11 nave-like spaces, delineated by a hypnotising trellis of striped double arches, built from alternating blocks of red brick and white stone. These arches were supported by hundreds of columns of marble, jasper and porphyry. There were also decorative flourishes in ivory, silver and gold, and mosaics and *azulejos* (painted tiles) made by master craftsmen. The effect was – and still is – astonishing.

Later extensions saw a new minaret added, the mihrab embellished, the outer aisles expanded. By the end of the tenth century, the Mezquita had grown to almost five times its original size, held up by 1,200 columns (around 850 remain). Then, on 29 June 1236, King Ferdinand III's Christian forces reconquered the city and everything changed. According to one account, the city's Muslims came to say their last prayers in the morning and, by that afternoon, a portable altar had been wheeled in for the first Catholic mass. The mosque was now a cathedral.

The process of Christianisation was undramatic until the 16th century, when King Carlos I – who hadn't seen the Mezquita – gave permission for a great chancel (the Capilla Mayor) and choir to be inserted into the heart of the building. However, when he visited for the initial unveiling, he was reputedly horrified: 'You have built here what you might have built anywhere, but you have destroyed what was unique in the world.'

The full cathedral took almost 250 years to complete. The result: a dissonant jangle of Gothic vaulting, Mannerist ceilings and opulent Spanish Baroque erupting from the calm simplicity of the Moorish prayer hall. Chapels dedicated to the likes of St Paul and the Souls of Purgatory have been slotted in. The original minaret has been wrapped in a bell tower – though while its faith and form may have altered, its function remains the same: it continues to call the devout to prayer.

Mass is held daily within the Mezquita – now officially known as the 'mosque-cathedral of Córdoba'. Muslim worship has been banned. But, despite this, the building does not belong to the Church, nor to any political body, organisation or individual. It belongs to everyone. And visitors of any or no religion can be touched by the calmness, the beauty, the history and the tenacity of this sacred place.

What?	Ancient island from which a disgraced prince converted a country to Christianity

Where?	Inner Hebrides, Scotland, UK

ISLE OF IONA

IT'S JUST the spot to commune with the heavens. Gazing westwards off this tiny isle – a flimsy drop of green in a gust-frenzied sea – you might believe there's nothing else in the world. Nature is all-encompassing and elemental: silvery sands, swelling surf, a scatter of rocks and skerries disappearing to an infinite horizon. The sky broods and grumbles, as if sending a message down from on high. And it does: rain. Lots of it. A deluge that spatters the waves and dances with the wind. Angry spirits? Or Scottish weather? It's been said that on the Isle of Iona there's 'only a tissue separating the material from the spiritual'. So perhaps it's both ...

Iona is an island on the edge, sitting just off the Isle of Mull, which itself sits just off the coast of Scotland. Sail west from here and it's next stop Canada. Yet this outpost of only 9 square kilometres (3½ square miles) possesses a power disproportionate to its remote location and diminutive size. Spirituality seems soaked into its very soil.

The bedrock of Iona dates back over 1,500 million years. It's some of the oldest rock in the world, imbuing the island with a raw, primal power. Scottish poet William Sharp once noted that to tell the story of Iona 'is to go back to God, and to end in God'.

The island has been considered sacred for centuries. Its old Gaelic name is Innis nan Druidhneach (Island of the Druids) – it's thought Druidic priests from England may have settled here to escape the Roman invasion. Then, in AD 563 an Irish prince named Columba washed up here. Columba had founded monasteries in his homeland. But he'd become engaged in a

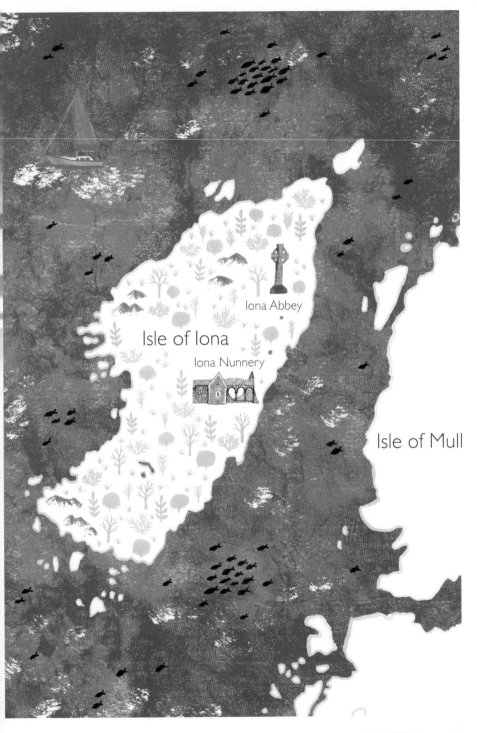

Isle of Iona

Iona Abbey

Iona Nunnery

Isle of Mull

row with another abbot over the copying of a manuscript, and it somehow escalated into a bloody war. The 'Battle of the Books' resulted in thousands of deaths and, as a result, Columba was banished from Ireland. So he set off in a coracle with 12 followers, bound for Scotland. He resolved to convert as many pagans to Christianity as had perished in the conflict.

Columba arrived on Iona, at the southerly cove known as Port na Curaich (Port of the Coracle). He climbed the island's highest point – 101-metre (331-feet) Dun I – and, satisfied that Ireland was no longer in sight, decided to settle. Columba built a simple church, which became known as a centre of learning. And, from this base, he headed out and set up camps (so-called 'colonies of heaven') among the local heathens, hoping to draw them to his faith.

Columba died in 597, the same year Benedictine monk Augustine arrived in England from Rome, sent to convert the pagan Angles to Roman-style Christianity. However, even after his death, Columba's Celtic way continued to spread.

In 802, Iona was razed by Vikings; Columba's remains were dispersed and the surviving monks retreated to Ireland. In the 12th century an abbey was built on Iona, with a nunnery alongside. These were abandoned and left to crumble when Scotland broke with the Papacy in 1560, leading to the Scottish Reformation. It wasn't until the early 20th century that restoration began. In 1938 the Reverend George MacLeod founded the Iona Community, an ecumenical Christian organisation committed to social justice that brought together young ministers and unemployed craftsmen to help rebuild the medieval complex. The community remains active today.

Pilgrims still flood to Iona. Nothing of Columba's original building remains, though you can trace the footprint of its boundary walls. However, you can enter the restored medieval church; you can visit St Columba's Shrine, the abbey's longest-standing structure, dating from the ninth century; and you can walk the Street of the Dead, a medieval trail leading to St Oran's Chapel and the graveyard where ancient Scottish kings – including Macbeth – were allegedly laid to rest. You can also breathe in the breeze atop Dun I, looking across Iona's hummocks and pastures, sea cliffs and stone remains, and feel the spirit of the place seeping into your soles.

What?	Mysterious Neolithic landscape of stone circles, man-made hills, ancient avenues and massive tombs
Where?	Wiltshire, England, UK

AVEBURY

WHAT EARTHLY purpose this mound might have served has been lost in the mists of time. It's such an unnatural-looking hump, bulging amid the pastures like an extraterrestrial beacon. But then, this whole landscape has an air of the not-of-this-world. As well as Silbury Hill – the largest man-made mound in Europe – the picture book English pastoral of Avebury is dotted with oddities: a mysterious sanctuary of concentric rings; a Neolithic avenue scything the fields; a village dissected by a mighty stone circle. So many secrets concealed in rock and earth. You climb to a tomb that dates back almost 6,000 years. Two hippies sit by its entrance, twirling wheat and singing to Mother Nature. You duck inside, run your hands over the ancient slabs and, for a moment, swear you hear Mother Nature singing back ...

The landscape around Avebury is profoundly English and profoundly old. The village here has all the countryside-quaint requirements: thatched pub, stately home, Saxon church. But it also has the world's biggest stone circle slicing through its middle.

The grassy chalk-hewn bank and ditch of Avebury Henge is around 1.3 kilometres (just under a mile) in circumference. Within that stands a huge ring of stones, which itself encompasses two smaller inner circles. It's believed the site was built between around 2850 BC and 2200 BC. The stones – sandstone sarsens, quarried a few miles away – measure up to 6 metres (19½ feet) tall and can weigh over 40 tonnes/tons. There were 98 in the larger circle alone (though only 27 remain). Shifting and erecting these monoliths, and excavating the mighty ditch must have

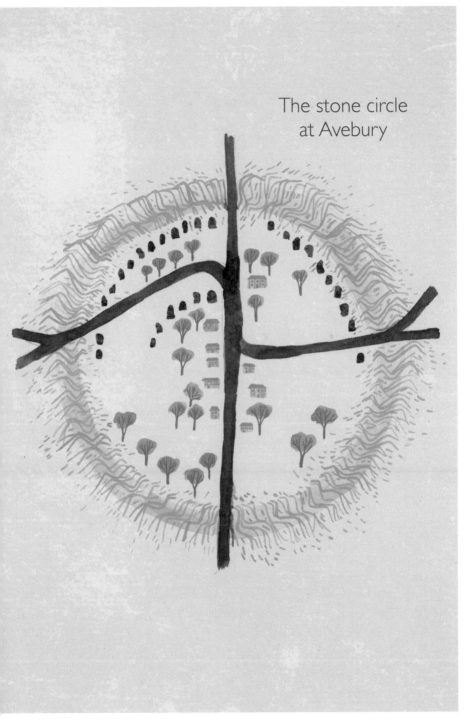

The stone circle
at Avebury

required not only superhuman effort but also a powerful motivation: why go to all this bother? No one knows, but theories abound. The more outlandish reckon Avebury was built by Druids or Native Americans or to mark the final battle of legendary King Arthur. More likely Avebury was one of England's principal Neolithic ceremonial sites. How worship worked here is unknown, but the moulding of the landscape suggests this was a theatre for public rites and rituals, where people expressed their relationship with the seasons, the spirits and the whole world order.

There is something undeniably compelling about this patch of England. Wiltshire is home to arguably Europe's greatest concentration of prehistoric monuments, and people have been drawn here for millennia. Some say our ancestors were acutely attuned to the planet's magnetic forces and picked this spot for its geo-magical properties. Avebury is supposedly a nexus of earth energy, with invisible ley lines (energy pathways) connecting it to other ancient sites such as the stone circle of Stonehenge, a short distance to the south.

When visiting, spend time within Avebury's Stone Circle, where there are no barriers to exploring the mammoth menhirs. Lay your hands on the Swindon Stone, the biggest, which marks the circle's north entrance and is the only stone never to have toppled. Then follow West Kennet Avenue, a ceremonial route once flanked by hundreds of sarsens. The grass here almost echoes with the footsteps of those who followed this processional 4,000 years ago. The avenue leads towards 39-metre (128-feet) high Silbury Hill, a man-made mound that was gradually added to over time. Archaeological excavations have found little inside. Maybe it was a sacred site, an observatory or a colossal compost heap?

Just beyond Silbury is West Kennet Long Barrow. Built around 3650 BC, this Neolithic burial mound is almost 100 metres (328 feet) long and contained the remains of at least 45 people. To enter the inky passage and squint into the empty chambers is a brief but chilling foray into the ancient underworld. From the barrow, you can walk to the Sanctuary, where the post-holes of a 4,500-year-old wooden structure – possibly a temple – are marked on the grass, and from where the Ridgeway, the so-called 'oldest road in Britain', leads off across this enigmatic land.

What? Magical medieval
monastery teetering on
a tiny tidal isle

Where? Normandy, France

MONT ST-MICHEL

OH, HOW those weary pilgrims must have felt when this titan hove into view. How their hearts must have soared as high as the island top itself after their long trudges across country and quicksand. Not even Walt Disney could have created a more fairy-tale feast for the eyes: Mont St-Michel, a pyramidal rock outcrop, higgle-piggled with houses of half-timber and stone, that rises to a mighty monastery and a heavens-piercing spire. Around it lies a sludge of mud and sand that, twice a day, is consumed by enormous tides, cutting the island off from the rest of civilisation. A division both physical and metaphysical; a demarcation of the human and spiritual worlds ...

Mont St-Michel sits just off the Normandy coast, at the mouth of the Couesnon River. Once known as Mont-Tombe (Tomb Mountain), this striking chunk of rock was first sacred to the Celts, who believed it to be a portal between earth and the afterlife. Christian hermits arrived around the sixth century, but the island's fortunes really changed in AD 708 when Aubert, bishop of nearby Avranches, had a vision in which the Archangel Michael instructed him to build a sanctuary on Mont-Tombe. Aubert ignored him. But the angel would not be deterred. He returned twice, burning a hole in the bishop's skull with his finger in order to convey the seriousness of his request.

So Aubert set off for the Mont. He'd been told that the exact spot on which he should locate his church would be indicated by a stolen bull; he found the beast right at the mount's summit, 88 metres (289 feet) above the sea.

Mont St-Michel didn't get off to a great start. Viking raids saw the first monastery destroyed several times. However, the Normans took control of the region in the mid-tenth century, and in 966 Benedictine monks settled, marking the official founding date of the abbey. Gradually a magnificent Romanesque monastery took shape, though with difficulty. The complex had to wrap itself around the island's pointy pinnacle of solid granite; supporting crypts were carved to create a platform for the church, and every room had to slot into the contours of the hill. The whole north side – church, choir, nave and tower – collapsed just decades after completion and had to be rebuilt.

Slowly a village grew up below the abbey. And soon pilgrims were visiting in their thousands. The island was considered a representation of Paradise on earth, and the faithful would come to seek the assurance of eternity from St Michael, archangel of judgement, weigher of souls.

Many modifications have been made to the Mont since its founding. In the 15th century the Romanesque chancel was given a Gothic overhaul; also ramparts were added to defend against English attacks during the Hundred Years' War. During the French Revolution the abbey was secularised and turned into a prison. But in 1966, a thousand years after the official founding, monastic life on the mount resumed. A small religious community continues to live in the abbey today.

From the mainland, it's a 2.5-kilometre (1½-mile) walk or bus ride to reach Mont St-Michel. Entry is via the Porte de l'Avancée, the right-hand of the two main gates, which leads into the bustling Grand Rue. This is the village's main street, which cuts between half-timbered houses touting touristy trinkets.

A steep staircase climbs to the abbey entrance. Inside are the grand Gothic-vaulted church and the monks' living quarters, known as the *merveille* (the marvel), a labyrinth of halls, cellars and corridors propping up the abbey above. From the top there are fine views over the bay, which is home to some of the world's biggest tides: up to 15 metres (49 feet) at their peak and, according to author Victor Hugo, 'swift as a galloping horse'. Surging waters, sea mists, sucking sand – the Mont could be a treacherous place for medieval pilgrims. But they came regardless, willing to risk it for a trip to Paradise.

What?	Catholic sanctuary based on a spring first revealed by a vision of the Virgin Mary
Where?	Pyrenees, France

LOURDES

PEACE, PRAYERS, faith, hope, the gurgle of a tiny spring ... All seem to echo around the crowded cavern. There are throngs of people yet no push 'n' shove; just an overriding calm as the quiet queue inches from bright daylight into the shadowy cleft ahead. There are people of all shapes and ages. Some process with eyes part closed, threading rosary beads through their fingers; others smooth the cool rock walls with their hands, as thousands – no, millions – of pilgrims have done before. Some carry candles or selfie sticks; some whisper or weep. Tucked into a niche above this hallowed cave, a marble statue of the Virgin Mary gazes down. It's said this is where she appeared on her visits to a young girl more than a century ago. Now she is there for all to see; for all to bask in her seraphic glow ...

On 11 February 1858 Bernadette Soubirous had a vision. This impoverished 14-year-old girl, born to Christian peasants in the small market town of Lourdes, was collecting firewood by the banks of the River Gave de Pau when something stirred nearby. A breeze tickled the leaves above a little grotto and a white-robed lady of incomparable beauty appeared. Bernadette was afraid – but entranced. She began to pray. After 15 minutes the female phantasm disappeared.

Over the following six months Bernadette had eighteen apparitions. During one encounter, the mysterious lady instructed her to drink at the spring, even though there was no spring to be seen. Bernadette pawed at the ground and eventually hit rising water; this sacred source has been flowing ever since.

QUE SOY
ERA
MMACULADA COUNCEPCIOU

The young girl was not widely believed. However, during Bernadette's 16th apparition, the lady revealed her identity: 'Que soy era Immaculada Concepcion'. When Bernadette relayed this to the local bishop, he was taken aback. He knew that four years previously the Vatican had ruled Mary to be of Immaculate Conception – something that uneducated Bernadette would not have known. This was taken as evidence of divine intervention. In 1862 the Catholic Church decreed the teenager's apparitions were real. The Virgin Mary had come to Lourdes.

Fame-shy Bernadette didn't hang around. In 1866 she left Lourdes to become a nun in Nevers, near Paris. She died in 1879, aged just 35, and was made a saint in 1933. Her supposedly 'incorruptible' remains, still looking fresh, are on display in a casket at Nevers' Chapel of St Gidard. However, she certainly left her legacy in Lourdes. Over 200 million people are thought to have visited this town in the foothills of the Pyrenees since the 1860s; during pilgrimage season (Easter–October) around 25,000 people visit each day.

The Sanctuary of Lourdes encompasses multiple churches, from the tiny Crypt (the original chapel) to the Church of the Immaculate Conception, with its exquisite stained-glass windows depicting Bernadette's 18 visions. But most come to visit the Grotto of Massabielle, or Cave of the Apparitions, where Bernadette saw Mary, and where the spring still gurgles inside.

To take advantage of these allegedly healing waters, pilgrims drink or splash themselves at the Lourdes fountains. Alternatively, they visit one of the site's 17 baths to fully submerge. Here, pilgrims must strip out of their clothes and dip into the glacially cold pools in only a simple white cloth. Attendants are on hand to help, and worship with them: 'Our Lady of Lourdes pray for us, St Bernadette pray for us'. Thousands claim to have been healed by these magical waters, though to date only 69 cases have been recognised as official miracles by the Lourdes' Bureau of Medical Observations. In truth, most people who go to Lourdes do not actually seek supernatural cures. They go for prayer, guidance and understanding; to unite with others of faith. They go not for physical therapy, rather to have their spirits healed.

WITTENBERG CASTLE CHURCH

THE BIG bronze doors are firmly shut, looking tough and impenetrable. You'd certainly struggle to knock a nail into them these days. Fortunately there's no need: the letter Martin Luther once pinned to this historic portal (which was then made of wood) is now inscribed into the metal itself, resistant to weather and wear; permanent, uneraseable. Inside, the church is elegantly simple: light floods through vibrant stained glass and the organ's boom resounds off the walls. You walk down the aisle to the choir and pause by a stone tomb topped with a plaque: 'Here lies the body of Martin Luther, Doctor of Divinity'. It might also read: Martin Luther – priest, composer, translator, revolutioniser of Western religion ...

Martin Luder was born in the Saxon town of Eisleben in 1483. His upbringing was tough under disciplinarian parents who were fiercely ambitious for their son to become a lawyer. Luder began to study but, in July 1505, while returning to university in Erfurt, he was caught in a thunderstorm. A lightning bolt struck close by, and he swore to the heavens that he'd become a monk if he survived. Survive he did. So, true to his word, and to his father's fury, he entered the Augustinian monastery in Erfurt. Some 18 months later he was ordained as a priest.

In 1508 Luder enrolled at the monastic school in Wittenberg. A year later, he graduated and began teaching theology. This is when his reformist thoughts started formulating; he became increasingly disillusioned with the Catholic Church's 'indulgences' – a system by which you could buy your way out of the

Germany

Wittenberg

Eisleben

Eisenach

Leipzig

Erfurt

Mainz

Worms

punishments of Purgatory, with the money going to the Papacy to fund fine cathedrals and Vatican renovations.

In 1517 Luder changed his name to Luther (from the Greek *eleutheros*, meaning 'freed') and he wrote his '95 Theses', which he tacked to the door of Wittenberg's Schlosskirche (Castle Church). This subversive document questioned the legitimacy of indulgences. For example, Thesis 86 asked: 'Why does the Pope, whose wealth today is greater than the wealth of the richest Crassus [the richest man in Roman history], build the basilica of St Peter with the money of poor believers rather than with his own?' It was a revolutionary letter. The Church was annoyed. Luther was summoned to Worms by the assembly of the Holy Roman Empire, and made the long journey to the city from Wittenberg (a route now known as the Lutherweg 1521 hiking trail). At Worms, he refused to recant and was excommunicated. But he continued to spread the word and ultimately sparked the Protestant Reformation – a shake-up of the Christian world.

Wittenberg's Schlosskirche, which sits at the western end of the medieval city, soaring above the meadows by the River Elbe, was only completed eight years before Luther pinned his missive to its entrance. Constructed as part of an opulent castle, the church was originally ringed by a moat, with bridges leading to the doors. However, in 1760 the building was badly damaged by fire. The church was rebuilt, and further restored over the years. In 1858 the new bronze theses doors were installed within the original stonework of the north portal. In the later 19th century, both the church and its tower were remodelled in a Neo-Gothic style.

Visiting the church, you can pay your respects at Luther's tomb. Nearby is the final resting place of his friend and collaborator Philipp Melanchthon, another key Protestant reformer. The church is open daily for services, concerts, tours and visits. It's also possible to climb the 289 steps up the round tower, which is inscribed with the title of one of Luther's hymns. Luther was a keen musician and believed music was essential to evangelical worship. He once wrote, 'next to the Word of God, the noble art of music is the greatest treasure in the world'. To sit in this church when its chamber choir and 19th-century organ are sending their songs soaring up to the vaults is perhaps the best way to appreciate Luther's legacy.

MOUNT OLYMPUS

THE HOME of the gods? Seems about right. This lofty realm of raw rock crags rising right out of the sea has a drama befitting the Ancient Greek pantheon. What better stage for their human–divine soap opera of incest, infidelity, murder and betrayal? However, there appear to be no deities in residence on Mount Olympus now as you make the final push to the top. It's been a testing climb, via fruit trees, lush forests, a riot of wildflowers and a flurry of butterflies. But now you're skirting the last jagged ridge and ahead is the flag that marks the summit. The weather gods are being kind – Zeus hasn't unleashed his thunder – and now you stand at the zenith of this sacred mountain under a burning-blue sky. You feel on top of this world, and perhaps a little bit closer to the next ...

Soaring 2,917 metres (9,570 feet) up from the waters of the Thermaic Gulf, Mount Olympus is the highest point in Greece. It's also the most legendary of mountains, central to the divine stories of the Ancient Greeks.

The tale begins millennia ago, when Cronus was the leader of the Titans, the older gods descended from Gaia (the earth) and Uranus (the sky). Cronus fathered many children with his wife (and sister) Rhea. But he'd been told he was destined to be overthrown by his own son, so as a precaution he swallowed each child as soon as it was born. Rhea was increasingly displeased with this. So, about to give birth again, she fled to Crete, hid her new baby – Zeus – in a cave, and gave Cronus a rock bundled in swaddling clothes to swallow instead.

Zeus grew up with an axe to grind. When he reached manhood he managed to free his siblings from Cronus's belly and started the Clash of the Titans, an epic battle for the privilege of ruling the universe. The old guard were led by Cronus and based on Mount Othrys. The young pretenders were led by Zeus and later became known as the Olympians because, after emerging victorious, they chose Mount Olympus as their HQ.

On the mountain, each of the Dodekatheon, the 12 Olympian gods and goddesses, had their own palace. Mytikas, the very highest peak, was their meeting place; the humped rock of Stefani was Zeus's throne.

Olympus began as a mythical mountain, a metaphorical representation of power and authority. Certainly Homer's epics, the *Iliad* and the *Odyssey*, offer few clues to its actual location. But more latterly the name (meaning 'luminous one') became attached to a specific peak. Mount Olympus – a massive massif, visible from Greece's second city of Thessaloniki on a clear day – was the obvious candidate for the divine abode.

Mountains as large as Olympus are much like gods anyway. They can inspire both fear and wonder, and draw people with a sort of effortless spirituality. Over the centuries, the mountain's rugged flanks have offered safe haven to those fleeing persecution, society, conflict and the law. Hermits have hidden in its caves and forests. People have made sacrifices and offerings at its sacred groves and on its highest pinnacles.

These days it's mainly hikers exploring Olympus's heavenly environs. You could take a walk around Dion, a sacred city located at the base of Mount Olympus. Dating from at least the fifth century BC, it's home to a large Temple of Zeus.

Or tackle the moderately strenuous summit circuit, which can be made in two or three days from the town of Litohoro. First you walk through the mountain's verdant lower reaches before entering the higher regions of bare rock and plunging ravines. There are refuges up here where you can stay overnight and watch the sun rise over the sea below. You might not actually bang into Apollo or Aphrodite while you're here but you can commune with those gods in spirit at least.

What?	One of the oldest Christian monasteries, at the foot of a biblical mountain
Where?	Sinai Peninsula, Egypt

ST CATHERINE'S MONASTERY

THIS LAND certainly feels biblical. The stiff climb has proven well worth it, for now you stand on the mountaintop at dawn, watching the sun creep up to set the world aglow. All around you lies a sprawl-rise-ripple of primordial rock, grey granite slabs and blood-red swells baked by a billion days. Sinewy tracks scored by centuries of hoof treads and footsteps creep across the wilderness, the only indication of life in this deserted desert, all heat and dust. The scene is rugged and raw, ancient and eternal. It could be another planet. It could be old as time. A fitting stage, then, for the appearance of the Almighty ...

Egypt's Mount Sinai is one of the most venerated spots in the Jewish, Christian and Islamic worlds. It was on the slopes of this 2,285-metre (7,497-feet) peak that God is said to have spoken to Moses as a burning bush, and where He delivered the Ten Commandments. According to the Bible, Exodus 19, there was a terrifying tempest, 'thunder and lightning ... thick cloud ... and a loud trumpet blast ... Sinai was covered with smoke, because the Lord descended on it in fire ... the whole mountain trembled violently. As the sound of the trumpet grew louder ... Moses spoke and the voice of God answered ...'

There's no archaeological evidence to back this up. And some theologians believe the Bible's Mount Sinai is actually Mount Al-Lawz in Saudi Arabia; others that it's a hill in southern Israel. However, Egypt's peak – also known as Jebel Musa (Moses' Mountain) – has staked the strongest claim.

Certainly as early as the third century AD the first monastics started coming to the Sinai region, longing to feel closer to God in this place of solitude and silence. In 311 Emperor Constantine ended the persecution of Christians, and in 330 a small chapel was founded at the site of the burning bush, in a narrow valley, high up in the desert.

However, it was in the mid-sixth century that the place prospered. Emperor Justinian ordered the building of a great basilica, enclosed in defensive walls. Since then the fortunes of St Catherine's – officially, the Sacred Monastery of the God-Trodden Mount Sinai – have fluctuated. This hallowed spot has witnessed the Muslim conquest, the discovery of St Catherine's bones (interred here around AD 800), peaks and troughs of pilgrims, the Crusades and the Arab–Israeli conflict. But still the monastery lives on.

Today a handful of Sinaitic brothers live here. They're awoken by 33 tolls of the church bell before dawn, they eat in the restored 11th-century refectory, spend their time in prayer, and celebrate feast days in the ancient basilica. Visitors are welcome most mornings, admitted via a small gate in the 3-metre (10-feet) thick ramparts. At one end of the complex is an evergreen bramble, supposedly a transplanted descendant of the actual burning bush. The original site of the sacred shrub is marked by a silver star in a screened-off chapel within the great basilica itself. Most other areas of the monastery – such as the 11th-century mosque and the extensive library (containing a collection exceeded only by that of the Vatican) – are out of bounds to outsiders. However, you may get a glimpse inside the charnel house, where masses of monks' bones sit in a gruesome pile. You might also see the Well of Moses, at which Moses met the seven daughters of Jethro, as recorded in Exodus; the water is still used by the monks today.

Many visitors come here simply in order to leave: St Catherine's is the start point for the pilgrimage up Mount Sinai. It's around a three-hour ascent from the monastery, with many hikers setting off in star-spangled darkness, hoping to reach the summit for sunrise. The path winds up via a cypress tree that marks where the prophet Elijah allegedly heard the voice of God. Then it's a trudge up 750 steps to the top, for that endless, timeless panorama. You may or may not be called by the Almighty, but the heavens do feel close enough to touch.

What?   Fulcrum of an ancient city
that is central to three
world religions

Where? Jerusalem, Israel

TEMPLE MOUNT AND OLD JERUSALEM

IS ALL the world wandering these hallowed streets? As you weave through Jerusalem's Old City, a walled warren of pale limestone, you're swept up in a sea of sartorial diversity: yarmulkes and tunics, tasselled shawls, monastic robes, hijabs, jeans and baseball caps. The air is rich with spices, incense, baking bread and the dust of ages. Muezzin calls from the minarets mix with chiming church bells, bar mitzvah celebrations and a multitude of languages – people of all nationalities chatter, chant and pray in their own ways. Jerusalem means so much to so many of differing faiths, and of none. It's a political powder keg, but also a concentration of devotion. Pilgrims are drawn by varying doctrines, but they're drawn here all the same ...

Jerusalem has a long history. It's thought the first settlement on this Judaean mountain plateau was founded around 5,000 years ago, making it one of the world's oldest cities. Over subsequent millennia, it's been battered, besieged, captured and recaptured multiple times, and even twice destroyed. But Jerusalem has proven to be a survivor. And it has continued to be a major pilgrimage destination, sacred to the three major monotheistic religions: Judaism, Christianity and Islam.

For Jews, Jerusalem – specifically Har HaBayit (Temple Mount) – was pivotal to creation. According to the Talmud, this raised area in the Old City is where God scooped up the earth from which Adam was made; it's also said to have been where rituals were performed, including Abraham's near-sacrifice of his son Isaac. King David erected an altar here, and the First Temple

was built by his son, King Solomon, in the tenth century BC. This was destroyed by Nebuchadnezzar, King of Babylon, in 586 BC. A Second Temple was built soon after, though this was razed by the Romans in AD 70. Now, all that remains is the Western Wall. But the Mount continues to be the holiest site in Judaism; Jews the world over face towards it when they pray.

For Muslims, Temple Mount is Al-Haram ash-Sharif (the Noble Sanctuary). It's the third holiest site in Islam, from where the Prophet Muhammed supposedly made his night journey to heaven. Soon after the Islamic conquest of Jerusalem in AD 637, the Al-Aqsa Mosque and dazzling Dome of the Rock were constructed here, the latter a resplendent shrine built atop the very slab – the Foundation Stone – from which the Prophet allegedly ascended. This is the same slab, says Judaism, on which Abraham made his sacrifice.

Christians believe Jesus regularly visited Temple Mount. He healed and preached there. He also dared challenge its corrupt authorities, which led to his death. His last supper was taken in Jerusalem; his last prayers were made at Gethsemane, just outside the city walls; he was crucified at Golgotha, now marked by Jerusalem's Church of the Holy Sepulchre, which houses Jesus's tomb.

Today Jerusalem jangles with multi-faith voices and religious tensions – security checks and armed police are the norm. But the spirituality of the place remains. Jews focus their prayers on the Western (Wailing) Wall; many refuse to step on Temple Mount itself for fear of desecrating the site's sanctity. However, modestly dressed visitors of all faiths are permitted to the complex. Entrance is through the Mughrabi Gate, which leads into a calm, open plaza dotted with ablution fountains, graceful arches and cypress trees. In the middle is the Dome of the Rock, its golden roof and exquisite blue-green tile work sparkling in the sunshine. Only Muslims may go inside.

Beneath the Dome is the hallowed Foundation Stone. And, beneath that, the Well of Souls (Bir al-Arwah) or Holy of Holies – a cave where (depending on your beliefs) the voices of the dead can be heard awaiting judgement, John the Baptist was annunciated or the Ark of the Covenant may be stored. So many stories and legends, so much faith and suffering, sunk deep into the earth.

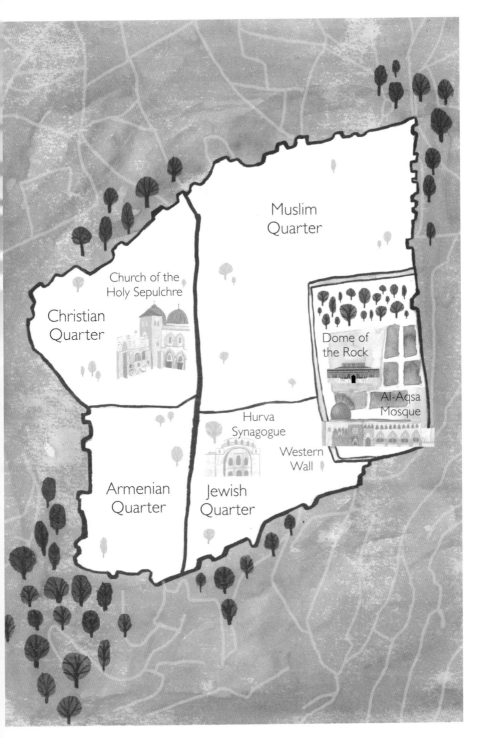

What?	Former Imperial capital city, and enduring cultural nexus
Where?	Honshu island, Japan

KYOTO

YOU'VE STEPPED across the threshold, from the world of humans to the world of the spirits; from the profane to the sacred. Ahead, a corridor of crimson *torii* – traditional Shinto gateways – snakes off and upwards, so close packed you can scarce see the trees on either side. It's like a red vein tethering the temples of Fushimi Inari Shrine to the mountaintop, to earth itself. You're flowing through an umbilical cord, being drawn back into the womb of Mother Nature. You climb, passing gate after gate, each inscribed with elegant black *kanji* characters – the prayers of benefactors who've bought a gate and, they hope, their good fortunes. Smaller shrines, stacked with miniature *torii*, nod to devout visitors with less deep pockets. Eventually, the density of gates thins. The view opens up. There is a city down below: Kyoto, once called *Heian-kyō*, Capital of Peace and Tranquillity. Kyoto has been the centre of Japanese culture for more than a thousand years – and remains its spiritual heart ...

In the late eighth century AD, Kammu Tennō, 50th emperor of Japan, relocated his seat of power to escape the increasingly oppressive Buddhist monasteries of Nara, Japan's original capital. After a brief move to Nagaoka (quickly deemed inauspicious), Kammu settled on what is now Kyoto in 794.

The location was ideal. Mountains flanked the northern corners, natural defenders against evil demons. The Kamo and Katsura Rivers provided the east and west boundaries; these joined the Yodo River, which ran south, linking the new capital

to the coast. A grand, planned city was built, with a central walled palace, and a network of intersecting thoroughfares and lanes. The population exploded. Soon, Kyoto was overflowing with temples and shrines, and drawing the best craftsmen, calligraphers, *kabuki* dancers and *ikebana* masters (flower arrangers). The city reigned for over a thousand years. Then, in 1868, the capital was moved from Kyoto to Edo (now Tokyo). But the best of the best of Japanese culture was – and still is – found here.

Despite over a millennium of battles, fires and earthquakes, Kyoto is one of the best-preserved cities in Japan. Not least because it was spared from World War II air raids – and worse. Kyoto was originally the US military's preferred atomic bomb target, but Secretary of War Henry Stimson argued the city was of too great a cultural importance to take the fatal hit. Today, more than 2,000 religious sites, including 1,660 Buddhist temples, 400 Shinto shrines and 90 Christian churches, are tucked amid its ancient lanes and modern sprawl. It is a city that has moved with the times, but in which the spiritual pulse of Japan beats loudest.

Founded in AD 711, Fushimi Inari Shrine and its photogenic trail of red *torii* is dedicated to Inari, the Shinto *kami* (god) of grains and fertility. It sits on the outskirts of Kyoto, a good spot to take in the whole city, and pay your respects. There are various ways to pray at Shinto shrines, such as burning *osenko* (incense), writing your hopes on wooden *ema* (wishing plaques) or saying a prayer while sounding the temple bell, thus alerting the spirits to your wishes. A *temizuya*, a small fountain, is found near the entrance of shrines and temples. Visitors should wash their hands and mouths, using the *shakushi* (bamboo ladles) to purify themselves before entering the grounds.

How to choose which other sacred spots to visit? Perhaps start with some of the 17 that have been designated UNESCO World Heritage Sites. Go early to Kinkaku-ji to see the gilded temple and surrounding trees reflected in its garden pond. Mull over the mysterious rocks of Ryōan-ji's Zen *karesansui* (dry gravel garden). Admire the five-storey pagoda of Tō-ji – the tallest wooden tower in Japan. And realise it would take around about a thousand years even to scratch the surface of this ancient sacred city.

| What? | Holiest and most dazzling of pagodas, housing eight of the Buddha's hairs |
| Where? | Yangon, Myanmar (Burma) |

SHWEDAGON PAYA

YOU CAN hardly look: this is Buddhism at its most blinding. The central spire of Shwedagon Paya sears into the hot, dark sky with the sparkle of a thousand Christmases, its slathering of gold and gemstones igniting the night. You feel like this hilltop vision must be visible for miles, maybe even from outer space. But what is the purpose of all this glitter? Buried beneath is a casket said to contain eight hairs from the head of Siddhartha Gautama, the Buddha himself. So, a precious monument for a most precious treasure. Myanmar's holiest site ...

The history of Shwedagon Paya is a little vague. According to legend, the pagoda complex is around 2,500 years old. It's said that around the fifth century BC, two merchant brothers met a recently enlightened Siddhartha Gautama, who gave them eight of his hairs, each eight finger-breadths long. The brothers returned to Myanmar, where they decided to enshrine the sacred strands on Singuttara Hill, already home to the relics of three previous Buddhas – the water filter of Kakusandha, the robe of Konagamana and the staff of Kassapa. A chamber, filled elbow-deep with jewels, was built to house all the artefacts – though when the hairs were transferred, there was 'a tumult among men and spirits': lightning flashed, winds blew, the deaf heard, the dumb spoke. To keep this power contained, a gold-coated slab was placed on top of the chamber, and a golden pagoda erected on top of that. This was encased in a succession of other pagodas made respectively of silver, copper, bronze, iron, marble and brick. However, it fell into disuse and was lost for hundreds of years.

Well, that's one story. Actually, archaeologists believe Shwedagon Paya was first constructed between AD 500 and 1000, with various tweaks made over the following centuries. It was in the 15th century, under the reign of Queen Shinsawbu, that the custom of gilding Shwedagon began – the monarch donated her weight in gold, which was turned into leaf and painted on the stupa. Her son then offered four times his weight, plus the weight of his wife. People continue to give gold to the temple – there are donation boxes specifically earmarked for the leaf, which is reapplied every year.

The complex standing today is the result of an 18th-century rebuild, following an earthquake. Four stairways lead up Singuttara Hill. Then four *zaungdan* (covered walkways), each guarded by *chinthe* (half-lion, half-dragon creatures) and lined with stalls and flower sellers, lead to the main terrace. This sweep of smooth marble is strewn with small pavilions, statues and shrines. And at its centre is Shwedagon, a 98-metre (322-feet) high *zedi* (bell-shaped monument) rising from a plinth and topped by an ornamental *hti* (parasol) that's encrusted with 5,448 diamonds, 2,317 other gems, 1,065 golden bells and one 76-carat diamond. Note, be sure to walk around the *zedi* clockwise, as is Buddhist tradition. Also, shoes must be removed.

The base of the *zedi* is surrounded by stupas: four large, marking the compass points; four medium, at the plinth's corners; and sixty small, around the edge. There are also planetary posts, representing days of the week; many worshippers make a beeline for the shrine that relates to their day of birth, where they light a candle, leave offerings and pour water on the Buddha image.

Despite its heavyweight holiness, a visit to Shwedagon Paya is not a solemn affair. For many people, going to the temple is a social as well as a sacred outing. The complex is especially lively from sunset: watch the last rays sink over Yangon and the river, then explore in the cooler evening, when the lights shine and the votive candles flicker. It's a place to be impressed by the bling but also soothed by the easy comings and goings of chattering friends, crimson-robed monks and those at peaceful prayer.

What? Holy mountain for
multiple faiths, topped
by a sacred footprint

Where? Central Highlands,
Sri Lanka

ADAM'S PEAK

THE STEPS seem to go on and on. And on. A never-ending climb that tugs at lungs and limbs. But, despite this, there's an irresistible momentum pulling you uphill in the lamp-lit darkness. You're part of a stream of human toil. The night air bubbles with spiritual songs, *sadhus*' chants and a whiff of the spicy *chai* being brewed alongside the trail. As dawn approaches, fatigue levels increase but the mood – just like the altitude – gets higher and higher. Your goal is nearing: at the zenith of Adam's Peak in Sri Lanka's lush tea country is the *sri pada* – a mysterious 'sacred footprint' that draws devotees of multiple religions. They come to worship at this holy rock and to watch in awe as the perfectly pyramidal peak casts its shadow onto the plains below ...

Adam's Peak is Sri Lanka's number one pilgrimage destination. On the top of this 2,244-metre (7,362-feet) conical mountain is a rock bearing a long, wide dent – a sacred footprint that has been appropriated by many faiths.

The early Sinhalese believed the mountain was the home of Saman, one of Sri Lanka's guardian gods who was later adopted as a Buddhist *bodhisattva* (enlightened being); the resplendent yellow butterflies that flock to the mountain in their millions are called *samanalayo*, in his honour. Today, Saman's main shrine lies in the village of Ratnapūra, from where the toughest pilgrimage route up the peak begins. Another Saman shrine guards the sacred footprint at the summit.

Buddhists believe the holy sole mark was created by the Buddha, Siddhartha Gautama. It's said that, on Gautama's third

visit to the island in the fifth century BC, he stepped on Adam's Peak with his left foot, and then strode right across the Bay of Bengal, leaving the indent of his right foot in Thailand. The print's great size – roughly 1.8 metres (6 feet) long – is down to the fact that the Buddha was supposedly over 10 metres (33 feet) tall.

According to Hindus, however, the impression was left by Lord Shiva as he danced the world into being. Christians say the mark was made by St Thomas, one of the 12 apostles, who introduced the religion to Sri Lanka. A 15th-century text claims the footprint was made by Pangu, the first man of Chinese mythology.

Muslims think the *sri pada* is the indent of the Prophet Adam, who landed here on one foot after being thrown out of Paradise, and had to stand that way for a thousand years as penance. The abundant gemstones – topaz, rubies, garnets, sapphires – found in the mountain's foothills are the crystallised tears shed by Adam and Eve after their banishment.

The footprint was allegedly discovered by exiled King Valagambahu in the first century BC, who was led there by a deity in the guise of a stag. Pilgrims of all creeds and classes have been visiting ever since, including legendary travellers Ibn Battuta and Marco Polo. Today, thousands climb Adam's Peak each year. Most come during pilgrimage season, from December to May, when the route is illuminated by a string of lights and the weather is driest.

There are four trails, which wend via tea estates and Buddhist shrines into the untamed realms of the mountain's wilderness sanctuary. There are testing sections, steep steps and long drops. *Ambalama* – wayside resthouses – have been built for pilgrims and travellers to stop, eat and sleep en route.

But eventually the summit appears, along with the small temple in which the footprint sits. Devotees prostrate before the sacred rock, touch it with their foreheads and make votive offerings: food, money, coils of silver. Some scoop out rainwater that's collected in the holy hollow, as it's believed to possess healing powers. Outside the temple, the view is magnificent. All of Sri Lanka seems to spread out – the ripple of the Central Highlands, the distant blue of the Indian Ocean. It's a place where many people feel closer to their gods, whomever those gods may be.

What?	Holy city on the holiest river, where Hindus flock to wash away their sins
Where?	North India

VARANASI AND THE GANGES

THE WATER in that river has come a long way. Those peripatetic droplets have dashed from the icy heights of the world's highest mountain range. They've swept via hundreds of miles of leafy foothills, cow-ploughed farmland, tiny villages and swarming pilgrimage centres on their way to the steamy Indian plains. And now this holy river has arrived in Hinduism's most sacred spot: Varanasi, the City of Light, allegedly founded by creator-destroyer god Shiva. Varanasi is where the devout come to bathe, believing the Ganges' blessed flow will wash away their sins. The pure hope to become purer; the impure hope to attain purity, temporarily at least ...

The River Ganges springs from the Gangotri Glacier in the high Himalaya and discharges into the Bay of Bengal after a journey of over 2,500 kilometres (1,550 miles). It's India's most sacred waterway; so revered, in fact, that it has become the first non-human entity in the country to be granted the same legal rights as people: in the eyes of the law, harming or polluting the Ganges is now equivalent to abusing a person.

For the majority of Indians, the river is a goddess in water form. According to Hindu mythology, Ganga was ordered to descend from the heavens to purify the mortals down below. Reluctant to do so, she became enraged, and vowed to wash away the world. However, Lord Shiva – the only deity strong enough to tame the mighty goddess – intervened. He received Ganga in his matted hair, tempering her fury and releasing her waters onto the earth in gentle streams.

Pakistan

Varanas

India

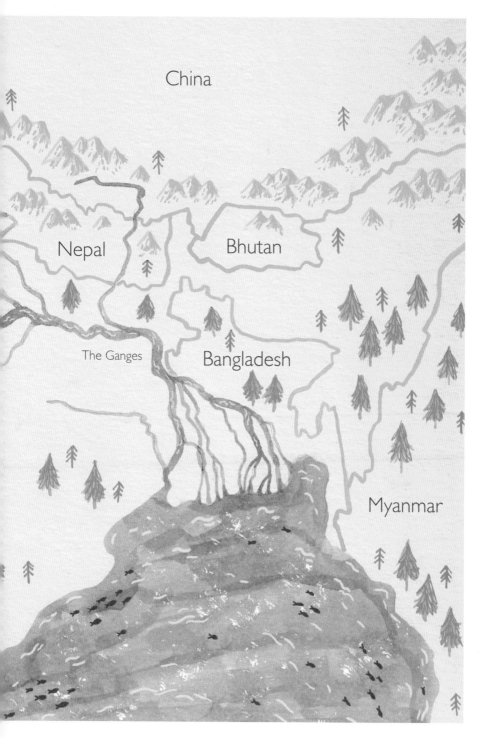

China

Nepal

Bhutan

The Ganges

Bangladesh

Myanmar

Varanasi, which sits on the left bank of the Ganges in the state of Uttar Pradesh, is among the world's oldest living cities. One legend states that it's where Shiva and his wife Parvati were standing when time first started ticking. Also called Kashi (Luminous), Varanasi is one of the holiest *tirthas* – spiritual crossing places that allow humans to access the divine and gods to descend to earth. As such, pilgrims have been flocking here for millennia in search of salvation and nirvana. Every Hindu hopes to visit at least once to take a sin-absolving swim. Jains also consider Varanasi sacred, while Buddhists make for nearby Sarnath, where the Buddha delivered his first sermon in around 530 BC.

Varanasi is a chaotic muddle of narrow weaving alleyways, ashrams and palaces, bullock carts, rickshaws, jewellery sellers and silk weavers. It's said there's a temple every ten steps, the most sacred being the golden-domed Vishwanath Temple. This is home to an ancient *lingam*, the phallic symbol of Shiva; on certain holy days, Hindus queue for hours for a chance to touch it.

However, most of the action in Varanasi is focused on the Ganges itself. Along the water's edge are numerous *ghats* (stone stairs) that lead down into the river. This is where you'll find devotees performing *puja* (prayers), kids flinging cricket balls and flipping somersaults, old men chewing blood-red betel nut, stretching *yogis*, ladies washing rainbow-bright saris and long-haired *sadhus* chanting mantras into incense-thick air. These steps give bathers access to the holy water. They lead up to crumbling palaces and temples. They host boisterous festivals. And they deal in death: Varanasi is considered an auspicious place for Hindus to die, and some *ghats* are reserved especially for cremations. At these sites, bodies are burnt on wooden pyres, the smoke drifting up to the heavens before the ashes are collected and scattered into the holy water.

One of the most atmospheric times to take to the river is at dawn. After haggling with a boatman, you can float down the Ganges as the rising sun warms the *ghats*, the temples and the monkeys scurrying in between. There's a sense of calm; the silence is broken only by the slow lap of the oars, the chirruping of birds and the bells chiming for the early morning rituals. Watch as this ancient city wakes up, and its circle of life and death, absolution and liberation begins again.

MOUNT KAILASH

THE SKY is a cloudless brilliant blue. A herd of yaks, hairy and cantankerous, crests the barren brow ahead while prayer flags flap in the wind. Nearby, a man drops to his knees, chanting softly as he prostrates for the umpteenth time. And there, at the centre of it all, is Mount Kailash – isolated, unmistakable, enormous – erupting from the plateau like a rock-hewn temple, gilded in snow. You shiver, not only because of the cold air but also because of Kailash itself: physically formidable, spiritually unmatched. More than a mountain, it is a mandala, the navel of the universe, source of four of Asia's great rivers, sacred to billions of people yet visited by only a few. A pyramid of power. An unconquered peak. An absolver of sin. You shiver once more ...

Mighty Kailash, a lonely 6,714-metre (22,028-feet) peak in wild western Tibet, is four-times sacred.

In the animist Bon religion it is known as the Nine-storey Swastika Mountain – the south face bears a vertical gash across its horizontal layers that resembles the ancient good luck symbol. The Bon say the peak is the home of the sky goddess Sipaimen, and the centre of all spiritual power.

For Buddhists, Kailash is Gang Rinpoche – Precious Snow Mountain. It is the abode of the tantric deity Demchok, and it is where Buddhism displaced Bon as the principle religion of Tibet. According to legend, in the late 11th century the Buddhist sorcerer Milarepa and the Bon shaman Naro-Bonchung engaged in a superhuman skirmish to see who was most powerful. Neither prevailed, so they agreed to race up Mount Kailash.

While Naro-Bonchung ascended on a magic drum, Milarepa sat meditating below. But when the Bon had almost attained the summit, Milarepa overtook him, gliding up on the sun's rays.

In Jain cosmology, Kailash is Mount Ashtapada, where the founder of the faith, Rishabhadeva, attained nirvana. For Hindus it is widely regarded as Paradise, and the home of Lord Shiva. According to legend, the god of destruction and regeneration spends his time atop the mountain practising yoga and making love to his wife Parvati. Some traditions suggest the mountain is Shiva's *lingam* (phallus) while nearby sapphire-hued Lake Manasarovar, one of the world's holiest pools of water, is Parvati's *yoni* (womb).

The mythologies may vary, but devotees of all four faiths make the arduous journey here. They travel across the Tibetan plateau to the trailhead village of Darchen in order to complete a Kailash *kora* – a circular pilgrimage around the mountain, deemed the pinnacle of spiritual life. The trek is roughly 52 kilometres (32 miles); many do it all in one long day, others take two or three days. Some hardy souls prostrate all the way around: the pilgrim kneels down, lies full length on the ground, makes a mark with their fingers, rises to the knees, prays, and then crawls forward to the mark just made before repeating the whole motion. *Koras* completed thus can take two or three weeks. In Buddhist tradition it's believed that performing one *kora* will erase the bad karma of one lifetime, 12 are considered a set, 108 *koras* lead to full enlightenment.

From Darchen, pilgrims spin prayer wheels for luck, then hike off past mantra-daubed *mani* walls into an unravelling of raw, spectacular scenery. There are many holy places en route: *chortens* (Tibetan shrines) and hill-perched monasteries; rocks said to bear the imprints of Milarepa's feet; and sky-burial points, where pilgrims perform an act of death – such as pricking a finger – in the hope of a higher rebirth in the next life.

The *kora's* zenith is the 5,630-metre (18,471-feet) Drolma-la pass which is often snowbound, strewn with prayer flags – blue for the sky, white for air/wind, red for fire, green for water, yellow for earth – and breathtaking indeed. Those who die right here are said to attain instant nirvana. However, if you survive the climb, you should leave behind a cloth, so your own anxieties, burdens and wishes can be released into the wind.

What? Northerly headland
where oceans collide
and the Maori enter
the afterlife

Where? North Island, New
Zealand

CAPE REINGA

OFF THIS wild, wind-gusty promontory, the Tasman Sea and the Pacific Ocean collide. You can see their disparate currents smack and whirl, foam and eddy, a ruction in the deep blue waters. No wonder the Maori believe this to be the gateway to the underworld. Cape Reinga, or Te Rerenga Wairua – the leaping place of the spirits – is almost the northernmost extreme of New Zealand, and certainly feels like an end-of-days sort of spot. Waves crash, dunes billow, seabirds scream. A crag-perched lighthouse warns of the shore's treachery – many a ship has floundered here. While a lone tree, bent double by age and weather, marks the place where the deceased are said to shuffle off this mortal coil ...

At the beginning of the 13th century, when Genghis Khan was heading the Mongol Empire, the Inca were emerging in Peru and England's King John was signing the Magna Carta, New Zealand was still an unknown nowhere, far adrift in the Pacific Ocean, untrodden by human feet. The first to find it were intrepid seafarers from Polynesia, now known as the Maori, who arrived in their *waka* (canoes) from around AD 1250. The Maori have no written history, but their creation mythologies have been passed down via generations of storytellers, a rich canon that attempts to make sense of this strange, remote, fractious and fabulous archipelago.

According to Maori legend, in the beginning there was Ranginui, the sky father, and Papatuanuku, the earth mother.

They lay together in a tight embrace, with their many sons stuck in the darkness between them. One day the eldest sons decided to separate their parents so they would have space to move. Rongo, god of cultivated food, tried first. Then Tangaroa, god of the sea, and Haumia-tiketike, god of wild food, joined in. But Ranginui and Papatuanuku did not budge. Then Tane Mahuta – god of the forest, and strongest of the lot – stepped in. With his shoulders to his mother, he pushed at his father with his legs, prising the pair apart. Papatuanuku wept uncontrollably, her tears creating rivers and streams. She finally stopped, though continues to mourn: mists rising from the forests are said to be Papatuanuku's sighs for her husband's touch.

After the separation, Tane Mahuta began to wonder why there were no females around besides his mother. Searching for a wife, he found only non-human females and fathered only birds and plants. In the end, he decided to make a woman for himself, taking rich, red clay from Papatuanuku's *uha* (genitals), moulding it into a female form and then breathing life into his creation. He called her Hineahuone. Hineahuone and Tane mated, conceiving Hinenuitepo. Tane also lay with Hinenuitepo and their many offspring became the human race.

As time passed, Hinenuitepo started to question who her father was. One day she asked Tane, who told her that it was, in fact, him. Hinenuitepo was so ashamed that she ran away to Te Rerenga and leapt into the underworld. Her children would live in Tane's protection; she would care for them in the afterlife.

When Maori people die, a *tangihanga* (funeral ceremony) is held. This takes place at a *marae*, an important communal meeting house that is considered *wahi tapu* (a sacred place). The body lies in an open coffin and, over a period of around three days, mourners visit from far and wide to speak to the deceased about both their virtues and their flaws. Mourners also express their grief, crying, singing laments and telling the departed to return to Hawaiki – the underworld, from which all Maori are born, and to which they go back to after death; the place that is the origin of life itself.

The spirit then makes this journey, from wherever in New Zealand they lie. Their life essence is said to travel to the far north, sweeping up the coast. It will pass near to the Waipoua

Forest, home to the tree known as Tane Mahuta, a giant kauri (*Agathis australis*) estimated to have an age of between 1,250 and 2,500 years. Next, the spirit will skim along wild Ninety Mile Beach (actually only 64 miles/103 kilometres long) to the tip of Cape Reinga. Here, it will slide down Te Aka, a root of the wizened pohutukawa tree that's reputed to be 800 years old, and travel underwater beneath Te Ripo-a-Mauria-nuku, the powerful current at the collision of the oceans. This leads it to Manawatawhi (last breath), the largest of the uninhabited Three Kings Islands. The spirit climbs up to the island's highest point for a final look back at the world. Then it plunges into the deep, to return to Hinenuitepo's safe-keeping.

Its role in the life–death cycle makes Cape Reinga the most spiritually important site for New Zealand's Maori, a place of connection to all those who've gone before. As such, eating is not permitted here and you're asked to *toihu te whenua* – leave the land undisturbed. There's plenty to explore though, with walking trails of varying lengths wending all along the coast, taking in dramatic beaches and the scattered evidence of human settlement dating back centuries.

On days when the mist rolls in and the cloud hangs low, some Maori elders claim to be able to hear a strange high-pitched singing barely breaking the silence – the sound of the passing of the spirits. Other visitors may not hear the ancestors' call as they drive along the hard-packed sand of Ninety Mile Beach (officially part of the highway system) to reach Cape Reinga. But on a wild day, with the surf boiling under furious skies, it's easy to imagine the underworld is only a dive away.

What?	Mighty monolith in the Red Centre, rich in Aboriginal Dreamtime legend
Where?	Northern Territory, Australia

ULURU

ULURU RISES like a blood-orange iceberg from the Outback, at once both utterly out of place and central to everything. It's an enormous anomaly amid the flatness of red sand and spinifex grass; dropped from the heavens or risen from the abyss, perhaps? Or like a lonely giant squatting in a wilderness of scrub, snakes and kangaroos. But it's also a lodestone. Try to take your eyes off it. You can't. This hulking rock, which bull's-eyes the very middle of Australia, is magnetic, monumental, unignorable – not least when the lowering sun sets its rusty sides aflame. No wonder the Aboriginal people of Australia consider it sacred. How could this beast of sandstone not be as old as time itself ...?

For the Aboriginal people, who first came to Australia over 40,000 years ago, Dreamtime is the mythological 'golden age'. It's the crux of their belief system; their means of interpreting the world. Dreamtime is when the first ancestors were created. It brought the dawn of knowledge and the development of the rules and rituals vital for human survival.

According to Dreamtime stories, in the beginning the earth was a flat, dark, empty place. But there were beings asleep below the surface and, when they awoke, they burst through the planet's crust; the sun rose too, bringing light for the very first time. The ancestors – who were half human, half plants and creatures – roamed around, creating extraordinary features in the landscape through their ordinary activities. As they sang, fished, hunted and died, they made mountains, rivers, deserts and trees; they made wallabies and lizards, eagles and ants, fire

and water, moon and stars; they also made people. And once this work was done, they returned into the earth and fell back to sleep, worn out by all their world-building.

Uluru was formed by the ancestors during Dreamtime, and is arguably their most striking legacy. More than 1.6 kilometres (1 mile) wide and over 3.2 kilometres (2 miles) in length, it rises around 350 metres (1,148 feet) above the ground – though, like an iceberg, there's twice that bulk hidden beneath. One story says Uluru was gradually piled up by two boys playing about in the rain-sloshed mud. Another says that it's the remains of a great red kangaroo that the mighty Rainbow Serpent once vomited up because the animal was too old and tough to digest. Yet another suggests the rock is the outcome of a bloody battle between two ancestral tribes; it's said the earth itself rose up in grief, becoming Uluru.

The Anangu people are the traditional land owners of what is now Uluru-Kata Tjuta National Park. They ask people not to climb Uluru both because it is a dangerous ascent and because the rock has such cultural significance for them. Only selected male elders are supposed to undertake the climb. Instead, the best way to experience Uluru is by circumnavigating its base. A round-the-rock walk, a distance of around 10 kilometres (6 miles), reveals an unexpected array of crevices, cracks and fissures that scar this massive monolith. These, say the Anangu, are marks left behind by a colourful cast of mythical figures such as the Mala hare wallabies and Kurpannga, the spirit dingo. Rituals are still held by the pools, boulders and caves around the base.

Such a walk is in keeping with Aboriginal culture too. As the Dreamtime ancestors roamed the land, creating the world in their wake, they laid out songlines – pathways between the newly formed features. This network of sacred trails engendered a pilgrimage tradition and peripatetic sensibility that Indigenous Australians still follow. Every year, dictated by the seasons, Aboriginal people would embark on walkabouts along the songlines; as they travelled they sang and danced, evoking the old fables. These performances also acted as maps, containing directions for these unmarked routes. In that way, songlines have been passed down the generations so that Aboriginal people can still walk in the footsteps first trodden by their ancestor spirits, millennia ago.

What? Deep pool in a collapsed volcano, sacred to the Native American Klamath peoples

Where? Oregon, USA

CRATER LAKE

THE DUSTY trail switchbacks down the cliff face through a fuzz of hemlock, red fir and lodgepole pine. Visible in snatches between the branches is the most dazzling shade of blue: Crater Lake, its pure waters sparkling within their mountainous bowl. These days, the steep Cleetwood Cove Trail is the only way to reach the shores of this flooded caldera. But as you listen to the whistling chickadees and brace your knees against the descent, you think of the Native American Klamath peoples, who once undertook more treacherous vision quests here. Crater Lake was an important site for these traditional spiritual rites. Klamath men would run along the sheer caldera wall down to the lake; those who could reach the shore without falling were believed to possess higher spiritual powers. For the Klamath, Giiwas – their name for this mysterious pool – was both revered and feared, a place of peril and sacred significance ...

Around 7,700 years ago, Mount Mazama erupted in spectacular fashion. This lofty stratovolcano in the Pacific Northwest's Cascades Mountains blew with terrifying fury, shooting a column of hot gas and volcanic rock high into the air. Fragments of ash and white pumice fell back down, scattering for more than a thousand miles. Mazama then collapsed in on itself. The mountain's summit, so painstakingly built up from successive lava deposits over a period of half a million years, vanished in days. The resulting hole filled with rain

and snow, to a depth of almost 600 metres (1,970 feet), creating Crater Lake.

Or so the scientific story goes. The Klamath peoples, whose ancestors were living in Oregon's Cascades Mountains before Mazama blew its top, tell a different tale. They say that one day, Llao, Chief of the Below World and spirit of the mountain, came up from his home in the earth's belly and stood atop Mount Mazama. While surveying the land, he caught sight of a local chief's daughter and fell in love with her. He vowed to grant her eternal life if she would return with him, down below. She refused, and Llao became enraged. He surged up through the mountain, pelting fire and fury, and threatening to exterminate her people.

However, Skell, spirit of the sky and Chief of the Above World, took pity on the people, and set to defending them. Skell took his position on Mount Shasta, at the southern end of the Cascade Range, and the two chiefs waged a thunderous battle, slinging scorching rocks as big as hills. The earth quaked; red-hot molten rock flows coursed down the slopes; the people fled in fright. Two holy men offered to sacrifice themselves by leaping into the fiery pit. But Skell managed to force Llao back into Mazama. The next day, the mighty mountain was gone. All that remained was a large hole, which was filled by torrential rain. And that is how Crater Lake came to be.

No matter your preferred creation story, this astonishing body of water inspires, moves, hypnotises. Call it holy spirits. Call it 'geo piety' – the worship of powers behind nature. Call it the punch of overwhelming beauty.

The specialness of Crater Lake didn't go long unnoticed. In 1902, President Theodore Roosevelt signed legislation making Crater Lake the USA's sixth national park. It's the deepest lake in the country, one of the deepest in the world, and one of the clearest: there are no inlets or outlets, so no sediment sullies the blue. That doesn't mean it's empty, though. Crawfish, a lesser spirit and follower of Llao, is said to lurk here. This giant monster with extremely long arms can pluck unsuspecting souls from the crater rim and drag them down into the lake's deep, dark abyss ... Less malevolent is the Old Man of the Lake, a bleached-white and weathered hemlock log that has been floating upright in the water for more than a hundred years. Buoyant and untethered, the Old Man rides the winds around the lake, and has been known to move several miles in a single day.

If you fancy a swim, be warned: Crater Lake is rather cold – those following the trail down to Cleetwood Cove in their bathers should be prepared. Just past the jetty is a rock outcrop, prime staging post for jumping in. Most swimmers only manage a few, bracing, soul-cleansing minutes. For Native Americans, such a dip might be undertaken at night in an attempt to encounter the supernatural beings believed to live under the water.

Another option from the jetty at Cleetwood is to board a boat to Wizard Island. This small, symmetrical outcrop of volcanic flotsam floating in the caldera is a lava-encircled cinder cone, formed during the ancient eruption. Or, according to some legends, it is the decapitated head of Llao himself, which was cut off by Skell before the latter fed Llao's body to his own children; some say the lake was formed from Llao's children's tears after they realised they'd eaten their father's flesh.

Trips run across to Wizard Island during the summer months only. At this time, you can disembark at the boat dock and follow the trails. You can wend amid the hemlock and white bark pine, climb to the island's summit, look up to the crater rim encircling you like a geological hug, and feel the spirit power beneath your feet.

MAUNA KEA

UP HERE, on the summit of this far-flung, far-reaching mountain, the heavens feel close enough to touch. You've never seen such an array of stars, pimpling the inky-black like celestial acne; the most resplendent rash. Constellations flicker. The Milky Way streaks. The occasional spark shoots overhead at speed. All these stars, these distant memories of the universe, speak science. You know they're luminous balls of hot gas, held together by their own gravity, burning a gazillion years away. But knowing the astronomical reality doesn't make them any less magical. No wonder the Native Hawaiians who stood atop the wild, cinder-crusted slopes of Mauna Kea felt they were in the realm of the gods. Here, high above the ocean, head touching the sky, is a place where you might find your own *mana* (divine power); where you might feel the connections between heaven and earth ...

Mighty Mauna Kea soars some 4,207 metres (13,800 feet), the highest point of the Hawaiian islands. Its name means 'White Mountain', on account of the winter snow that dusts its lofty heights. But that isn't the half of it. From its base right down on the Pacific Ocean floor to its massive sky-nudging summit, Mauna Kea measures over 10,000 metres (32,800 feet), making it taller even than Mount Everest – and thus the highest mountain on the planet.

A relative baby in geologic terms, Mauna Kea – which is one of five hotspot volcanoes that form the Big Island of Hawaii –

was only formed a million years ago. A hefty sub-aqua eruption caused vast streams of lava to pour out of the seabed and stack up and up and up, gradually creating this gargantuan volcano. It wasn't until around 1,500 years ago that the first humans arrived – adventurous Polynesians in their seafaring canoes. Unsurprisingly, this massive mound looming out in the middle of the blue caught their attention and became embroiled in their tales of creation.

In the beginning, there were no written records of these myths. They were passed down orally. One version was the Kumulipo (translated as 'beginning in deep darkness'), a historic *mele oli* (chant) of over two thousand lines that recounts the Native Hawaiian creation story. It gives clues to ancient societal structures and documents the genealogy of key island chiefs. It was first printed in the late 19th century.

According to some legends, in a time long ago Wakea, the Sky Father, looked down and beheld the beauty of Papahanaumoku, the Earth Mother. He saw the ocean flow sinuously about her body, and bioluminescence sparkle in her waters, just like his stars. They married, and became the primordial parents: their love gave rise to all things, including the Hawaiian islands and their mountains, which they garlanded with *leis* of cloud and sea foam. Big Island was their *hiapo* (eldest child) and Mauna Kea was that child's *piko* (navel). So to Native Hawaiians, Mauna Kea isn't merely a volcano, it's *kupuna* (an ancestor); it's the centre of existence, the umbilical cord connecting the land to the gods.

Four female deities are said to reside on Mauna Kea: Poli'ahu, the snow goddess; Lilinoe, who controls the mist; Waiau, the angel of the underground water; and Ka Houpo o Käne, who represents the springs. One story tells how Poli'ahu was once sledding on the east slope of the mountain when a stranger challenged her to a race. Poli'ahu beat this mysterious figure twice but on the third run the stranger released molten lava in front of Poli'ahu, revealing herself as volcano goddess Pele. Poli'ahu dashed up Mauna Kea and threw snow at the fiery flow below, forever limiting the lava to Big Island's southern reaches. Even now, it's said Pele rules southerly Kilauea and

Mauna Loa – both active volcanoes – while Poliʻahu is boss of dormant Mauna Kea, further north.

Mauna Kea might not spit the flames and fury of other Hawaiian peaks but its upper slopes remain strange and alien. Indeed, Native Hawaiians consider it a place apart, and treat the summit area with reverence and caution. The world is, they say, divided into Wao Kanaka and Wao Akua – the zone of the people and the zone of the gods and spirits. The top of Mauna Kea is considered Wao Akua, and not a place for people to enter without purpose or forethought. The volcano is a house of worship created not by man but by the *akua* (gods), and governed by the laws of the heavens. It certainly looks otherworldly, with landscapes of sparse and hardy alpine tundra, black basalt, cinder deserts and often biting winds.

Mauna Kea is also dotted with specific *wahi pana* (sacred places) – '*wahi*' meaning 'place', '*pana*' meaning 'pulse', so literally 'places with a pulse', or living spaces. There are *heiau* (temples), *lele* (altars) and burial sites that Native Hawaiians implore you to respect. As such, visitors are asked not to hike to the top of the cinder cone that marks Mauna Kea's true summit.

Less spiritual are Mauna Kea's so-called 'golf balls', the bulbous, white astronomical observatories that dot the skyline, making the most of the high vantage and dry, clear skies to find out more about the universe – this is one of the best star-gazing spots in the world. Some people love these high-altitude scientific stations, some people hate them. Either way, they are certainly ensuring that this mountain maintains its connection between mankind and the skies.

What?	Enormous igneous rock poking from the prairie, sacred to Native American peoples
Where?	Wyoming, USA

DEVILS TOWER

AMID THE endless swaying grasslands and the deep green fronds of ponderosa pines, it suddenly appears. A curious colossus, with no apparent purpose or precursor, soaring from the prairie. Devils Tower is an oddity on all counts, out on its own, occupying a place where science, sci-fi and spirituality merge. Geologists don't know quite what to make of it – how exactly was this igneous intruder formed? UFO fans are convinced it's a beacon for alien craft (which, gazing up at the monolith right now, doesn't seem so far-fetched ...). But it's for the Great Plains peoples, who've long roamed this wilderness, that Devils Tower holds the greatest draw. This monolith is a sacred site that provides them with indelible connections to their ancestors, their culture and the natural world ...

Devils Tower, a 386-metre (1,267-feet) high thumb-up of rock protruding near Wyoming's Black Hills, is an astounding sight. When you look close you see it's less one rock than a big bunch of them – hundreds of hexagonal columns fused tight in an enormous bundle. While geologists argue over details (is it the remains of a long-gone volcano? Or the remnants of a laccolithic bulge?), they generally agree that the tower first formed around 55 million years ago, when a mass of molten magma intruded into the earth. Eons of erosion has since uncovered this cracked core, leaving it lonely and exposed on the rolling prairie.

Or so the scientists say. For the many tribes of the Great Plains region, including the Lakota, Arapaho, Cheyenne, Shoshone and Crow, Devils Tower has a quite different creation story.

One tale tells of seven young girls who were playing in the forest when they came across a gigantic bear. The girls ran for their lives, into the trees, but the bear gave chase and began to catch them. Terrified and desperate, the girls hopped onto a small, squat rock and began praying fervently: 'Rock, take pity on us. Rock, save us'. The Great Spirit answered quickly: the rock began to swell, surging higher and higher, carrying the girls up into the sky. The raging bear tried to follow, leaping up against the rising tower and scouring deep claw marks into its sides. But it couldn't reach. The tower kept growing until the girls were lifted into the safety of the heavens, where they became the seven stars of the Pleiades constellation. For the Lakota this is not Devils Tower. They call it Bear Lodge.

Indeed, the Lakota have arguably the strongest connections to this place. The Black Hills are their seat of creation, and they would come to Bear Lodge to fast, pray, make offerings and perform rituals. Shaman would conduct cleansing ceremonies and individuals would undertake vision quests here to seek spiritual guidance. One Lakota legend tells of a warrior embarking on such a quest at the base of Bear Lodge. It's said he suddenly found himself on the summit, with no idea how to get down. So he prayed to the Great Spirit, then fell asleep. When he awoke, he'd been returned to the ground. Also, it's said the Lakotas were given the White Buffalo Calf Pipe, the tribe's most sacred object, at Bear Lodge. The pipe was traditionally kept in a hidden cave on the tower's north flank.

Many tribes still use the land around Devils Tower for their rituals. Walk around the base of the butte, amid the pines, and you'll see bright scraps of cloth tied to the branches. These prayer offerings symbolise a connection to the site. They also echo nature's own colours. The tower, which became the first United States National Monument in 1906, sits within a national park rich in wildflowers, from yellow-flowering biscuitroot and white pussytoes to bluebells, purple mustard, scarlet globemallow and crazyweed. Though maybe the most impressive colour of all comes at sunset, when the day's last rays turn the tower bright red, and it really does feel like the aliens might have landed.

What?	Magic-infused cove where First Nations totem poles soar and sink back into nature
Where?	Haida Gwaii, British Columbia, Canada

S'GANG GWAAY

EYES CLOSED, you listen. The wind riffles the leaves, branches creak; gin-clear water tickles the shingle. But you don't hear the cries. S'Gang Gwaay, the Haida name for this faraway place, means Wailing Island; they say tides thrusting air through a rock hole create a sound like a weeping woman. But no, there's no wailing now, just a silence in which sorrow and spirituality hang as thick as the moss on the trees. The village here, huddled on a forest-backed cove, is long deserted yet seems to teem with ghosts. As grasses regrow over the rotting ruins, and as the weathered totem poles fall to the earth, there remains an unshakable connection between this land and the people who once called it home ...

Haida Gwaii, an archipelago of 150-odd islands laying across the Hecate Strait from the British Columbia mainland, has been inhabited by humans for millennia. It's thought the Haida, a North American First Nations culture, first settled in the area over 8,000 years ago. Their way of life was moulded by the islands' own rugged terrain, wildlife-abundant forests and rich seas. The Haida foraged for food and medicinal plants, fished what they needed, and felled selected trees to make canoes, build shelters or create works of art. However, they also understood that their survival depended on looking after these precious natural resources. They lived in harmony with the environment, knowing their role was not as land owners but land stewards. This philosophy or world view was called *Yah'guudang* – a respect for

all living things. It celebrated how Haida people and their spirits were inseparably intertwined with nature, and recognised the responsibility to protect the environment for future generations.

At its peak, the Haida population reached more than 14,000. But after European settlers arrived from the late 18th century, the number plummeted. By 1915 only 588 Haida remained. S'Gang Gwaay, in the far southwest corner of the archipelago, is a tragic case in point: the village here was abandoned in the 1880s after a devastating smallpox outbreak. But that's what makes a visit so poignant. Seeing the old longhouses rotting beneath the moss and the ash-grey totem poles in varying degrees of decay hints at the bond between the Haida and the land, and the wider struggles of First Nations peoples.

S'Gang Gwaay, which is also known as Ninstints – the name of the most powerful of the village's chiefs in the mid-19th century – is now UNESCO World Heritage listed, such is its cultural significance and the quality of its fine totems. In the absence of a written language, these sacred poles and their symbolic designs provided the Haida with reminders of everything from ancestral rights and social standings to myths featuring supernatural animals and birds. Hewn from enormous cedar trees, they were often carved with clan crests, which were key to Haida hierarchy.

Traditionally, Haida were separated into one of two moieties (groups): Raven, the mischievous trickster who is said to have released the first humans from a clamshell, or Eagle, the spiritual guide known for loyalty, strength and courage. These two moieties sub-divided into multiple lineages, each with its own crest – the Haida have almost 70 crests, taking in the scope of the natural world, from Killer Whale and Beaver to Dogfish and Horned Owl. Each lineage also has its own canon of myths, dances and songs, and its own rights to resources such as fishing spots, bird rookeries and hunting areas. A Raven had to marry an Eagle, while lineages were passed down the matriarchal line.

Most of the totems remaining at S'Gang Gwaay are mortuary poles, erected with great ceremony for the most important community members. A cavity in the top held a box containing the deceased's ashes, placed there a year after death.

A potlatch, or gift-giving feast, accompanied the erection of the totem poles. The word is a corruption from the Nootka Indian language, meaning 'to give away', and these ceremonies saw possessions gifted, or even destroyed, to display wealth and generosity, build ties in the community and enhance status.

The poles were not designed to last forever – and that is how the Haida wish it to be. While some of the site's poles were, controversially, removed to museums in the 1950s, those that remain are being left to their own devices, overtaken by lichen and salal, slowly returning to the earth.

S'Gang Gwaay is only accessible by boat. Tours sail along the wild, pristine coast of Haida Gwaii, skimming waters teeming with sea lions and whales, where bald eagles swoop overhead. On arrival, passengers disembark and meet the Haida Watchmen that guard the site. These First Nations guides lead tours, walking visitors through the great, green old-growth forest to the quiet little cove, conveying the ancient songs and stories entwined with the landscape. No more than a dozen visitors at a time are permitted, making it the most intimate of cultural encounters. And in the absence of the living, it's easier to feel the presence of the dead.

What? Mysterious ancient city,
       believed to be the origin
       of Mesoamerican
       civilisation

Where? Valley of Mexico, Mexico

TEOTIHUACÁN

TEOTIHUACÁN: THE birthplace of the gods. That's the name the Aztecs bestowed on this mysterious, long-abandoned city when they found its ruins sinking into the Valley of Mexico. It was a big claim. But, as you absorb Teotihuacán's improbable scale, it doesn't seem entirely unfounded. Standing atop the Pyramid of the Moon, with the gargantuan Pyramid of the Sun to your left and the die-straight Avenue of the Dead disappearing into the heat haze ahead, you feel awe. From up here the milling tourists appear as ants, made tiny by the city's vastness – though what's visible now is only a fraction of the original site. From up here you appreciate the ancient urban planning; you look out at the pathways, plazas and temples that intersect with what seems almost otherworldly geometric precision. From up here you could begin to believe Teotihuacán might be teetering on the divine ...

Sitting 50 kilometres (31 miles) northeast of Mexico City, Teotihuacán is an archaeologically striking site. But the greatest wonder of it is that so much is still unknown. Who built it, exactly when, and why, remain a mystery. It's thought a settlement was established here around 100 BC (though possibly much earlier), with the most impressive building work beginning from the first century AD. Teotihuacán then went on to become the greatest city of Mesoamerica, peaking around AD 450, with a population of 80,000 – some say over 200,000 – people.

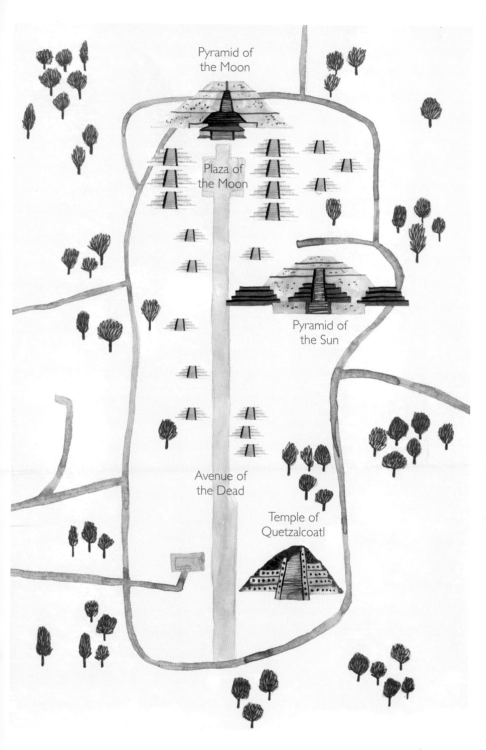

Pyramid of
the Moon

Plaza of
the Moon

Pyramid of
the Sun

Avenue of
the Dead

Temple of
Quetzalcoatl

But just a century later it started to decline, and many of its buildings were sacked and burned. Some historians blame an outside invasion; others an internal uprising, carried out by starving masses overthrowing the elite. Either way, the city was abandoned, its magnificent structures left to the elements, its identity lost to Father Time.

Despite its dilapidated state, Teotihuacán exerted a powerful influence over subsequent civilisations. For the Aztecs, who arrived a thousand years after the city's peak, it was a holy place – the very origin of civilisation. According to their legends, this is where the old fire god Huehuetéotl lit a sacrificial bonfire into which jumped two gods to create the 'fifth sun', thus beginning the present era. The Aztecs adopted much of the city's iconography, and Aztec king Montezuma made many pilgrimages here during his reign.

Teotihuacán does seem to have been laid out by some greater power – or at least a civilisation in tune with the universe. The structures are arranged on a cardinal grid, skewed 15.5 degrees and 16.5 degrees clockwise from north and east, tying in with a sacred solar calendar.

The Pyramid of the Sun is the city's focal point. Completed around AD 200, it's the world's third largest pyramid: its base, which measures 215 square metres (2,314 square feet), is almost exactly the same as Egypt's Pyramid of Cheops, though with its stepped sides reaching 'only' 65 metres (213 feet) high, Teotihuacán's monument is considerably shorter. Built of earth and adobe bricks, its sides were once coated with smooth lime plaster and vibrant murals. Its purpose is unknown, but directly beneath the pyramid's centre is a cave shaped like a four-leafed clover. It's possible that this was considered to be a royal tomb, a holy of holies or sacred womb of humankind, which may be the reason for the mammoth construction above.

The Pyramid of the Moon is smaller, but still striking. Its shape mirrors the contours of Cerro Gordo, the sacred hill looming behind, while its position on Teotihuacán's highest ground further increases its stature. Excavations here have unearthed tombs containing human skeletons, offerings of jade and obsidian, and the remains of sacrificial animals including puma and wolves. One of the latest archaeological discoveries is what is believed to be a secret tunnel running deep below the surface from the temple to the Plaza of the Moon. This large square is surrounded by 12 smaller stepped pyramids, allowing as many as 100,000 people to gather to witness sacrificial rituals.

Dissecting the site on a north–south axis, and connecting the main temples, is the broad Calle de los Muertos (Avenue of the Dead). This causeway measured around 4 kilometres (2½ miles) long and was named by the Aztecs, who believed the mounds and buildings lining the avenue were tombs; archaeologists believe they were actually temple platforms and palaces.

One of Teotihuacán's most impressive monuments is the Ciudadela, a royal residential complex incorporating a vast sunken square and the stepped, sculpture-adorned Temple of the Feathered Serpent. The Aztec later named this creature Quetzalcoatl – he was a major deity of ancient Mexico, and is thought to have first featured at Teotihuacán. More than 200 people are believed to have been sacrificed during the building and dedication of this temple, grouped and buried in seemingly strategic places for reasons unknown.

Teotihuacán's murals – often depicting gods, sacrifices and warriors – indicate its inhabitants were fearsome fighters; it's thought their aim in battle was not acquiring territory but taking prisoners who could be ritually killed to prevent apocalypse. Given the ultimate downfall of this remarkable city, it seems the Teotihuacán's bloodlust did them little good in the end.

What?	Jungle waterfall where bathers seek blessings from the Virgin Mary and vodou spirits
Where?	Haiti

SAUT-D'EAU

THE WATERFALL is heaving. There are people everywhere, clambering over slick rocks, standing in the vine-draped pools, tying strips of cloth to the overhanging trees. Some pilgrims recline in the shallows, allowing the cool current to flow over their bare chests; others wash themselves vigorously, rubbing at their skin with soap and torn leaves. One woman flails and wails with crazed eyes, her body possessed. Insistent drum thumps, trumpet blasts and hypnotic songs swirl with the water's constant rush. Candles burnt to the stub ooze wax over the boulders while bottles of rum are shared and swigged. Everyone seems intoxicated – though whether that's down to the potent liquor or the effects of the *Vierge Miracle* (Virgin of Miracles), who can say? The Catholic saint-cum-vodou deity is a powerful presence at this cascade, and all who bathe here hope for the goddess's particular brand of benediction ...

Haiti sways to the beat of its own drum. Occupying the western side of Hispaniola island (the Dominican Republic occupies the east), the country became the world's first black republic in 1804, after a successful revolution led to freedom from the French. But this landmark independence came after centuries of colonial rule, during which time slaves shipped to the Caribbean from West Africa were forced to convert to Catholicism. Their former religious practices – largely, the worship of a great pantheon of ancestor spirits – were banned and subsequently driven underground or

amalgamated with Christianity. African deities might be disguised as Catholic saints so they could still be worshipped; parts of the liturgy were appropriated to replace old-world prayers lost across the Atlantic. A smattering of traditions were even absorbed from the Arawak, the indigenous Caribbeans. The result: Haitian vodou – a sacred smorgasbord. Eclectic, syncretic, distinct.

Bondye is the supreme creator-god of this monotheistic hybrid religion. Named from the French *bon dieu* (good god), he is responsible for universal order and the fate of mankind. However, he is a remote being, too all-powerful for humans to interact with directly. Instead *vodouisants* (practitioners of vodou) pray to Bondye via the *lwa*, spirits that act as intermediaries between the god and humans, and that bring his will to the people.

There are three main families of *lwa*. *Rada lwa*, which have their origins in the religions of West Africa, are mostly kind and creative forces, and are associated with the colour white. *Petro lwa*, younger spirits with their roots in the New World and slavery, are harsher and angrier, associated with the dark arts and the colour red. *Ghede lwa*, whose colour is black, are linked to death and sexuality; they are responsible for carrying the souls of the deceased, but are known for being lewd, irreverent and cracking obscene jokes.

The festival held at Saut-d'Eau each July typifies Haiti's spiritual pick 'n' mix. This thundering waterfall in the island's jungly interior has been considered holy since 1849, when a female spirit allegedly appeared here alongside a tree. It's said that when this beautiful vision disappeared her image remained, imprinted on a palm leaf. When that leaf dropped, the image reappeared on another leaf. People started to come to see this supernatural phenomenon, leaving offerings and saying prayers.

However, the Catholic priests disapproved of such superstition, and one of them cut the tree down; it's said he died in unexplained circumstances later that day. When worshippers moved their attentions to a second tree, another priest chopped that one down; he also died soon after. Eventually a church was built in the nearby village of Ville Bonheur, which cemented the site's reputation as a place of miracles. Now thousands of devotees make an annual pilgrimage to the waterfall, to give thanks or pray for better fortunes.

The goddess who appeared in that 19th-century vision was the Virgin Mary of Mount Carmel; the festival climaxes on 16 July, the Virgin's feast day. But this Catholic icon has a vodou counterpart, known as Erzulie Dantor. Erzulie is the *lwa* of motherhood, a tough, dark-skinned warrior woman and supreme protector of children. She is often portrayed as the Black Madonna of Częstochowa, a painting brought to Haiti in the early 19th century by Polish soldiers fighting in the revolution. Some branches of vodouism depict her as a buxom lady with a scar on one cheek, a baby in one hand and a knife in the other. She is also the goddess of rivers, lakes and waterfalls, able to ease ailments of the womb. Thus many women come to Saut-d'Eau to give offerings of their undergarments in the hope of curing infertility.

The festival begins with a church ceremony in Ville Bonheur before a lively procession to the waterfall, led by Rara musicians. This is the typical Haitian music played to accompany processions; key instruments are *vaksen* (bamboo trumpets), drums, maracas and *güiro* (scrapers); songs are sung in Creole.

Once at Saut-d'Eau, pilgrims shed their outer clothes and perform a variety of rituals. Cloth strips, usually red/pink or blue (Erzulie's preferred colours), are worn around the waist then tied to branches by the waterfall; they are believed to rid the wearer of bad luck. Then, pilgrims bathe and dance, drink rum and coconut juice, light candles and use ceremonial gourds to pour water over their heads. Many hope for the ultimate blessing: to become possessed by the spirit of Erzulie herself.

What?	Ethereal high-altitude lagoon amid the mountains, believed to be where Inca life began
Where?	Eastern Peru and western Bolivia

LAKE TITICACA

A COOL breeze ripples the water's surface while the sun dazzles off it with blinding intensity. You've never seen such a brilliant blaze of blue: ultramarine lake meeting cobalt sky; an eye-searing onslaught of cyans and sapphires. A few little birds dart and chirrup among the stunted trees. A *tortora* reed boat floats lazily past, poled by a man in a bright woollen hat. Grassy hillsides and terraced fields fall down to the lake shore and, in the far distance, a wall of mighty mountains rears up to kiss the heavens. You gasp for air, unsure if it's the oxygen-poor altitude or the remarkable spectacle that's leaving you so breathless. Or perhaps it's because you're gazing over the very cauldron of creation ...

On the border of Bolivia and Peru, Lake Titicaca shimmers between the snowcapped Andes and the wild, windblown Altiplano at a breath-stealing altitude of around 3,800 metres (12,470 feet). It is vast – the largest lake in South America – measuring 190 kilometres (118 miles) long and up to 80 kilometres (50 miles) wide, with a maximum depth of 280 metres (919 feet). But it's much more than a set of impressive numbers. For some pre-Columbian peoples, Titicaca was the cradle of humanity.

Take the Inca, the civilisation that emerged here in around AD 1200 and quickly rose to rule much of the continent. One of the Inca's key deities was the creator-god Viracocha. According to their legends, when all was an empty void, Viracocha rose from Lake Titicaca and formed the earth and the heavens. He made animals. Then, by breathing life into

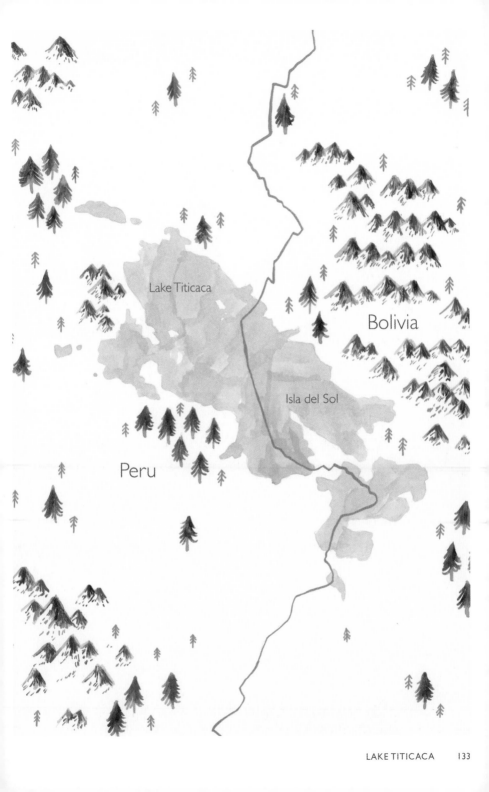

Lake Titicaca

Bolivia

Isla del Sol

Peru

stones, he fashioned a race of rock giants. However, because he failed to make any light, these giants lived in a state of dim-witted darkness. They began to annoy Viracocha. So he sent an almighty storm to wipe them out. Then he tried again, this time using clay to mould a new mankind, and bestowing on them gifts such as language, songs, clothes and agriculture. He also made new animals and plants. And he used the islands dotted on Lake Titicaca to create the celestial beings that would light up the world: from Isla del Sol he made the sun; Isla de la Luna the moon; Isla Amantaní the stars. His work done, Viracocha then set off dressed as a beggar to spread his knowledge far and wide.

But Lake Titicaca wasn't only part of the Inca's great creation myth, it was also central to the birth of their civilisation. One story says that the Inca founder-king Manco Cápac was brought up from the lake's inky depths by the sun god, Inti; another that Cápac emerged from a rock on the Isla del Sol. Consequently this Island of the Sun, on the Bolivian side of Lake Titicaca, became a hugely important religious hub. Thousands of pilgrims from across the Inca empire came to visit its shrines. As well as many temples, the island was renowned for its excellent maize. Pilgrims would return home with Isla del Sol grain to put in their own stores, believing it would ensure an eternally good harvest.

After the Spanish conquest, the island was looted and many temples were destroyed. But it remains a place of peace and spirituality. There is no motorised traffic, just a network of rocky trails leading between the small villages, tumbling farms and Inca ruins. The holiest site remaining is the Santuario, the now ruined complex housing *Titikala* – the Rock of the Puma. This slab of pink sandstone, after which the lake is named, is said to be where Viracocha created the sun. In Inca times, offerings of gold, feathers and shells were left here; sacrifices – both animal and human child – were made; elaborate ceremonies were held. Most common pilgrims weren't allowed into the complex's inner sanctum. Even after making arduous journeys across the Andes, they would only have been permitted to view *Titikala* from the *Intipunku* (Sun Door), the gateway to the sanctuary. But now anyone can walk right up to this sacred rock and put their hands where the light of the world began.

What?	Remote volcanic isle scattered with sacred sculptures in the form of mysterious huge heads
Where?	Pacific Ocean, off Chile

EASTER ISLAND

IT LOOKS like the aftermath of a grim celestial skirmish. The grassy slopes of this long dormant crater are strewn with hundreds of huge, haunting stone heads staring enigmatically into the sky. They're *moai*, and they're everywhere. Some stand erect, but others tilt at awkward angles, lie toppled and prone, or are sinking back into the ground. An army of great warriors, defeated and left for dead. Or a cemetery of the gods. You approach one of these giants, transfixed by its enormous aquiline nose, its heavy brow, its expression that seems to say ... what exactly? Hard to know. Just as it's hard to understand why a tiny group of people living out on the edge of the world went to the trouble of carving so many of these massive things. What purpose where they trying to fulfil? What gods were they trying to appease? And what on earth went so very wrong ...?

Far adrift in the Pacific Ocean, about 3,700 kilometres (2,300 miles) off the South American mainland, Easter Island is one of the remotest places on the planet. And one of the most mysterious. It's thought that this small, rugged chunk of rock, comprised of three extinct volcanoes, was first settled by intrepid Polynesians in their double-hulled canoes at some point between AD 400 and 800. According to legends, the first settlers came from the east, from the mythical homeland of Hiva. It's said that Haumaka, the royal tattooist, had a dream that his spirit ventured to a far-off island to find new territory for his king Hotu Matua; he called it Te Pito o Te Henua (the Navel of

the World). When Haumaka told the king, a search party was sent out. The mission was successful, so the king set off with his queen and crew in a canoe loaded with banana shoots, taro seedlings, pigs and chickens. After a six-week voyage, they landed on the white sand of Anakena Beach, on Easter Island's north coast. The royal residence was established there and the descendants of Hotu Matua (*matua* meaning 'father') are said to have ruled for a thousand years.

Quite how the peoples of Hiva managed such an epic voyage to such a tiny speck in the ocean is unknown. But even more intriguing is what they did after they arrived. As society developed on this isolated isle, these new colonisers – who became known as the Rapa Nui – started to sculpt. Using basalt *toki* (stone axes), they chipped away at the soft tuff, creating huge, strange statues. Ranging from 2 to 20 metres (6½ to 66 feet) tall, and weighing up to 40 tonnes/tons, almost 900 *moai* were carved at the crater of Rano Raraku. Many were then dragged across the island, to be erected by the sea on *ahus* (ceremonial platforms). Quite how these heavy heads were transported right across the island is yet another mystery. Legends attest that priests were able to move *moai* with *mana* (spiritual energy). More likely they used a wooden sledge and a lot of man power.

It's posited that the *moai* were part of an ancestor cult. The Rapa Nui believed their forefathers' spirits remained close long after death, and could be called upon to help in times of need. Thus when important clan members died, a *moai* would be hewn from the quarry and raised on an *ahu* facing the clan village to watch over the living. Some were also capped with a red scoria *pukao* (topknot) or inlaid with white coral eyes – by opening a statue's eyes, its inner force was ignited. The *moai* were *tapa* (sacred), a symbol of power.

Because *mana* was passed through *moai*, clans became fiercely competitive. If you could build a bigger statue than your neighbours, you'd have more good fortune; island wars even saw clans topple each other's *moai*. The whole community became obsessed with the statues, to the detriment of all else – with all the trees felled for moving *moai*, the Rapa Nui couldn't build canoes to escape their fast-degrading environment. And the statues that were supposed to provide protection were ultimately central to the Rapa Nui's fall.

Just getting to remote Easter Island is an adventure – it's a five-hour flight from Santiago, six hours from Tahiti. Once there you can explore the many *moai* sites. For instance, admire the 15 statues at Ahu Tongariki and the beachside sculptures at beautiful Anakena. Or take a walk around Rano Raraku crater, the Rapa Nui's wondrous outdoor workshop.

You can also learn about the curious *Tangata Matu*, or Birdman cult, which centred on creator-god Makemake. This became Easter Island's belief system after the island was denuded, the population tumbled and *moai* worship ceased. At this time, the only remaining source of food was migratory sea birds, and the main annual ritual saw the most important men on the island each appoint a *hopu* (young, lower-status man) to swim to the offshore islet of Motu Nui on their behalf in order to retrieve the first egg of the sooty tern. The winning patron was bestowed with gifts and gained high status. The *hopu*, on the other hand, was lucky to survive: many drowned, fell from cliff faces or were eaten by sharks.

Orongo, located on a volcanic caldera at the island's southwest tip, was the centre of Birdman worship. Visit today and you can still see the cluster of low, round, stone buildings that comprised the ceremonial village. And you can still look out to tiny Motu Nui, across the treacherous waves, and feel for the poor souls who had to make this strange and desperate journey.

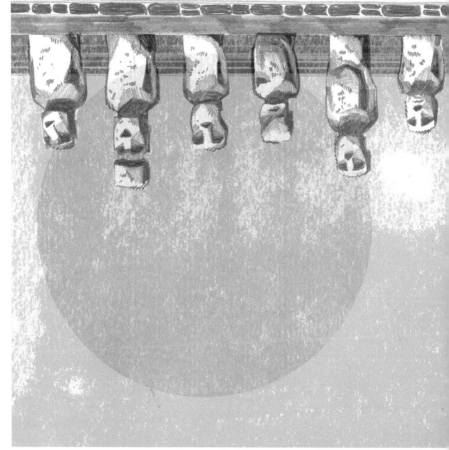

SARAH BAXTER grew up in Norfolk, England and now lives in Bath. Her passion for travel and the great outdoors saw her traverse Asia, Australia, New Zealand and the United States before settling into a writing career.

She was Associate Editor of *Wanderlust* magazine, the bible for independent-minded travellers, for more than ten years and has also written extensively on travel for a diverse range of other publications, including the *Guardian*, the *Telegraph* and the *Independent*. Sarah has contributed to more than a dozen Lonely Planet guidebooks and is the author of *A History of the World in 500 Walks* and *A History of the World in 500 Railway Journeys*.

HARRY & ZANNA GOLDHAWK are a husband-and-wife team who create their illustrations from their beautiful seaside cottage in Cornwall. As well as illustrating books, Harry and Zanna also run their own online business Papio Press, where they make gorgeous illustrated prints and gifts.